Southern Cooking

Made Easy for Your Everyday Meals

Les Ilagan

Copyright by CONTENT ARCADE PUBLISHING

All rights reserved.

This cookbook is copyright protected and meant for personal use only. No part of this cookbook may be used, paraphrased, reproduced, scanned, distributed or sold in any printed or electronic form without permission of the author and the publishing company. Copying pages or any part of this book for any purpose other than own personal use is prohibited and would also mean violation of copyright law.

DISCLAIMER

Content Arcade Publishing and its authors are joined together in their efforts in creating these pages and their publications. Content Arcade Publishing and its authors make no assurance of any kind, stated or implied, with respect to the information provided.

LIMITS OF LIABILITY

Content Arcade Publishing and its authors shall not be held legally responsible in the event of incidental or consequential damages in line with, or arising out of, the supplying of the information presented here.

Table of Contents

Introduction i

APPETIZERS 1
- Breaded Cheese Sticks 1
- Breaded Polenta Sticks 2
- Cajun Spiced Baked Potato Wedges 3
- Crunchy Organic Okra Bites 4
- Cumin Spiced Chicken Meatballs 5
- Breaded Cajun Shrimp 6
- Corn Fritters with Scallions 7
- Crispy Chicken Fingers 8
- Oven-Baked Chicken Meatballs 9
- Potato Fritters with Herbed Sour Cream 10

SOUPS 11
- Cream of Carrot and Pepper Soup 11
- Cream of Pumpkin Soup with Chili 12
- Hearty Broccoli and Corn Soup 13
- Pumpkin and Corn Soup 14
- Pumpkin Soup with Sour Cream 15

MAINS 16
- Classic Shrimp Po Boy 16
- Roast Beef with Pepper and Rosemary 17
- Crab Cakes in Lemony Tartar Sauce with Dill 18
- Cajun Spiced Grilled Chicken Breast with Honey 19
- Country Style Crispy Fried Chicken with Buttermilk 20

Pepper Crusted Cod Fillet with Paprika 21

Southern Fried Chicken Wings in Spicy BBQ Sauce 22

Spiced Chicken Drumstick with Thyme 23

Meat Potato and Cheese Casserole 24

Baked Turkey Meatballs with Spicy Yogurt Dip 25

Honey Mustard Chicken Roast 26

Savory Shrimp and Grits with Thyme 27

Tasty Buffalo Wings 28

Baked Honey-Mustard Drumsticks 29

Beef and Pumpkin Stew 30

Beef Stew with Polenta 31

Breaded Chicken Cutlets 32

Breaded Turkey Breast with Rosemary 33

Broccoli and Cheese Quiche 34

Cajun Shrimps with Herbs 35

Marinated Shrimps with Herbs 36

New Orleans Shrimp and Grits 37

Garlic Lime Shrimp with Paprika 38

Grilled Chicken Drumstick and Corn 39

Grilled Herbed Salmon 40

Grilled Marinated Salmon on Spinach Bed 41

Herbed Beef and Vegetable Stew 42

Herbed Chicken Burger Patties 43

Cheesy Vegetable and Rice Casserole 44

Chicken and Vegetable Stir-Fry 45

Crispy Fried Chicken Wings 46

Pasta and Chicken Sausage in Tomato Sauce 47

SIDES 48
Zucchini and Cabbage Casserole 48
Cheesy Eggplant and Tomato Casserole with Herbs 49
Homemade Vegetarian Casserole 50
Cheesy Mushroom and Potato Bake 51
Green Bean Casserole with Cheddar 52
Creamy Baked Macaroni and Cheese 53
Broccoli Pasta and Cheese Bake 54
Macaroni Mushroom and Cheese Casserole 55
Sweet Potato Casserole with Pecan 56
Easy Succotash Recipe 57
Steamed Vegetable Medley 58

SALADS 59
Creamy Potato Egg and Onion Salad 59
Garden Fresh Salad with Roasted Chicken Breast 60
Red Cabbage and Carrot Slaw with Mango 61
Coleslaw with Apple and Scallions 62
Fresh Green Salad with Smoked Salmon 63
Spinach Salad with Shrimp and Persimmon 64
Fresh Peach Salsa 65

SNACKS 66
Homemade Spinach Cornbread 66
Southern-Style Yellow Cornbread 67
Quick & Easy Choco Almond Scones 68
Pumpkin Scones with Raisins and Walnuts 69
Homemade Buttermilk Biscuits 70
Breadsticks with Parmesan and Herbs 71

Polenta Sticks with Cheddar 72

Homemade Buttered Corn Muffins 73

Egg Salad on Toasts 74

Homemade Chicken Nuggets 75

Turkey Bacon Muffins with Chives 76

Zesty Meatballs with Parsley 77

Egg on Avocado Boat 78

DESSERTS 79

Pecan Pie with Honey and Cinnamon 79

Ultimate Pineapple Upside-Down Cake 80

Homemade Peach Crumble Cake 81

Luscious Lemon Meringue Pie 82

Mississippi-Style Mud Pie 83

Easy Blueberry Cobbler Ala Mode 84

Gooey Pecan Tarts 85

Key Lime Pie Home-Style 86

Crispy Fried Apples with Cinnamon 87

Quick and Easy Banana Pudding 88

Blackberry and Cream Dessert with Honey 89

Watermelon Peach and Blackberry Salad 90

Chocolate and Vanilla Pudding 91

Baked Strawberry and Almond Crumble 92

Apple Cobbler ala Mode 93

Apple Fritters with Cinnamon 94

Baked Pumpkin and Caramel Pie 95

Banapple Fritters 96

Carrot and Walnut Cake 97

Choco Almond Cake 98

Choco-Hazelnut Cookies.. 99

Chocolate Avocado Pudding 100

Country-Style Pecan Pie 101

Creamy Pasta and Fruit Salad 102

Home-Style Apricot Galette.. 103

Peach Cobbler ala Mode 104

Les Ilagan

Introduction

The traditional Southern way of cooking food is basically a combination of elements from different cuisines such as English, Scottish, Irish, African, German, French, and Native American.

There are several types of Southern cuisine namely - Creole, Low country, Tidewater, Appalachian, Floridian, and the Caribbean.

At present, the fundamentals of Southern cuisine have expanded towards the north which influenced the development of other kinds of American cuisine.

The use of pumpkin, tomatoes, corn or grits were inherited from the south-eastern American Indian people. While, baked and dairy products such as bread, pies, and the use of different kinds of cheese came from European cuisine. Staples like okra, black-eyed peas, rice, eggplant, sorghum, and melons, as well as the use of spices, are associated with African origin.

Whether you are serving meals for the family or to your party guests, you will never run out of great ideas with this book. It is packed with delightful Southern recipes that are made simple that even beginners can easily follow. From classic recipes to contemporary recipes this book has it all.

It is a part of many cookbook series that I am writing, I hope you'll have fun trying all the recipes in this book.

Les Ilagan

APPETIZERS

Breaded Cheese Sticks

Preparation Time: 10 minutes; **Total Time:** 30 minutes; **Yield:** 12 servings

Ingredients
12 (1 oz. or 30 g) sticks cheese string
2 eggs, beaten
1 ½ cups (150 g) breadcrumbs, seasoned
vegetable oil, for frying

Method
1. Remove the plastic wrap on string cheese sticks and cut in half crosswise.
2. Place the eggs in a medium bowl and the breadcrumbs in a large shallow bowl.
3. Dip each cheese stick into the egg and then roll in breadcrumbs until completely coated; place all breaded cheese sticks onto a lined cookie sheet. Allow cheese sticks to stand at room temperature for 5 minutes. Dip in the egg again then roll into the breadcrumbs.
4. For a minimum of 2 hours, freeze the cheese sticks.
5. Heat oil in a deep-frying pan to high. Deep fry the cheese sticks until golden brown for 8 minutes.
6. Transfer into a plate lined with paper towels to drain excess oil; cool slightly.
7. Serve and enjoy.

Note: Avoid overcrowding of the cheese sticks in the pan by frying in batches.

Nutritional Information:
Energy - 184 kcal; Fat – 12.0 g; Carbs – 10.8 g; Protein – 9.7 g; Sodium – 329 mg

SOUTHERN COOKING

Breaded Polenta Sticks

Preparation Time: 10 minutes; **Total Time:** 30 minutes; **Yield:** 12 servings

Ingredients
2 cups (500 ml) whole milk
4 cups (1 L) chicken stock
2 Tbsp. (30 g) butter
3 ¼ cups (520 g) dry polenta
2 oz. (60 g) cheddar cheese, shredded
1 oz. (30 g) parmesan cheese, finely grated
1/4 cup (15 g) fresh parsley, chopped
salt and freshly ground black pepper
vegetable oil, for frying

Method
1. Combine the milk, chicken stock, and butter in a large saucepan; bring to a boil. Reduce heat to a simmer. Gradually whisk in polenta and continue cooking and stirring until polenta pulls from the edge of the pan.
2. Add the cheese and parsley. Season with salt and pepper to taste. Spread polenta evenly over a baking sheet and refrigerate until set.
3. Transfer polenta to a cutting board and cut into cut ¾ x ¾ by 3 ½ inch sticks.
4. Heat oil in a deep-frying pan to high. Next, fry the polenta sticks until golden brown.
5. Drain excess oil by transferring them in a platter lined with paper towels.
6. Serve and enjoy.

Nutritional Information:
Energy - 259 kcal; Fat – 10.2 g; Carbs – 35.0 g; Protein – 6.4 g; Sodium – 180 mg

Cajun Spiced Baked Potato Wedges

Preparation Time: 10 minutes; **Total Time:** 30 minutes; **Yield:** 12 servings

Ingredients
2 Tbsp. (30 ml) olive oil
2 tsp. (4 g) ground cumin
1 tsp. (2 g) ground coriander
1 tsp. (2 g) hot paprika
1 tsp. (2 g) ground turmeric
½ tsp. (1 g) dried oregano

½ tsp. (1 g) ground black pepper
¼ tsp. (0.5 g) chili powder
2 (40 g) egg whites, slightly beaten
2.2 lbs. (1 kg) potatoes, cut into wedges
cooking oil spray

Method
1. Preheat oven to 375°F (180°C).
2. Whisk together the olive oil, herbs, and spices in a large bowl.
3. In a separate bowl, place the egg whites then toss in the potato wedges first followed by the olive oil mixture.
4. Arrange the seasoned potato wedges in a single layer on a greased baking pan.
5. Bake in the preheated oven, about 30 to 40 minutes turning occasionally, until golden brown and crispy. Cool slightly.
6. Serve and enjoy.

Nutritional Information:
Energy - 156 kcal; Fat – 5.1 g; Carbs – 24.8 g; Protein – 4.0 g; Sodium – 123 mg

Crunchy Organic Okra Bites

Preparation Time: 15 minutes; **Total Time:** 40 minutes; **Yield:** 4 servings

Ingredients

1 lb. (450 g) of organic fresh okra, cut into small pieces
1 cup (175 g) cornmeal
1 tsp. (2 g) sweet paprika
½ tsp. (1 g) cumin, ground
1/2 tsp. (1 g) garlic powder
1/2 tsp. (1 g) onion powder
1/2 tsp. (2.5 g) Kosher salt
cooking oil spray

Method

1. Preheat oven to 400°F (200°C). Grease a large baking sheet with oil spray.
2. Combine the cornmeal, paprika, cumin, garlic powder, onion powder, Kosher salt in a bowl. Mix thoroughly.
3. Roll each okra in the cornmeal mixture, covering all sides. Place all covered pods on the prepared baking sheet. Bake for about 25 minutes, or until the okra bites are golden brown.
4. Serve and enjoy.

Nutritional Information:

Energy - 195 kcal; Fat – 8.2 g; Carbs – 28.6 g; Protein – 4.4 g; Sodium – 306 mg

Cumin Spiced Chicken Meatballs

Preparation Time: 15 minutes; **Total Time:** 40 minutes; **Yield:** 6 servings

Ingredients
1 lb. (450 g) ground chicken
2 (60 g) large eggs, lightly beaten
1/2 cup (50 g) dry breadcrumbs
1/4 cup (60 g) cream cheese
1/2 Tbsp. (3 g) garlic powder
1 tsp. (2 g) cumin, ground
1/2 tsp. (2.5 g) Kosher salt
1/2 tsp. (1 g) freshly ground black pepper
cooking oil spray
fresh parsley

Method
1. Preheat oven to 450°F (225°F). Slightly grease a baking sheet with oil spray.
2. Combine the ground chicken, beaten eggs, breadcrumbs, cream cheese, garlic powder, cumin, salt, and pepper in a large bowl. Mix well.
3. Take about 1 tablespoon mixture and form into small meatballs. Put them on a prepared baking sheet. Lightly spray with oil.
4. Bake in the preheated oven for about 18-20 minutes or until golden brown.
5. Transfer to a serving dish. Garnish with fresh parsley.
6. Serve immediately and enjoy.

Nutritional Information:
Energy - 279 kcal; Fat – 14.3 g; Carbs – 11.5 g; Protein – 27.8 g; Sodium - 507 mg

SOUTHERN COOKING

Breaded Cajun Shrimp

Preparation Time: 12 minutes; **Total Time:** 30 minutes; **Yield:** 6 servings

Ingredients
1 lb. (450 g) shrimps, peeled but tails left intact
2 tsp. (4 g) Cajun seasoning
1 cup (125 g) flour
1 cup (100 g) panko breadcrumbs
2 (60 g) whole eggs, lightly beaten
canola oil, for frying

Method
1. Heat enough oil in a deep frying pan.
2. Using a paper towel, pat shrimps dry. Season with Cajun seasoning.
3. Coat with flour, dip in egg, and then roll in panko breadcrumbs to coat.
4. Drop each breaded shrimp in the pan and fry until golden brown.
5. Transfer to a serving dish.
6. Serve with your favorite dipping sauce.

Nutritional Information:
Energy - 339 kcal; Fat – 13.0 g; Carbs – 30.1 g; Protein – 23.6 g; Sodium – 337 mg

Les Ilagan

Corn Fritters with Scallions

Preparation Time: 12 minutes; **Total Time:** 30 minutes; **Yield:** 8 servings

Ingredients
1 cup (175 g) yellow cornmeal
1/2 cup (60 g) all-purpose flour
1 tsp. (4 g) baking powder
1/2 tsp. (2.5 g) kosher salt
1/4 tsp. (0.5 g) freshly ground black pepper
1 pinch nutmeg
1 (60 g) whole egg
1/2 cup (125 ml) milk
1/4 cup (15 g) scallions, chopped
1/2 tsp. (1g) paprika
6 oz. (180 g) canned corn kernels (reserve ¼ cup liquid)
canola oil, for frying

Method
1. In a medium bowl, mix well cornmeal, flour, baking powder, salt, pepper and nutmeg.
2. In a large bowl, beat the egg; then add the reserved corn liquid and milk.
3. Whisk the flour mixture into the liquid mixture to blend well.
4. Stir in corn and scallions. For best results, refrigerate the batter for 30 minutes.
5. In a large frying pan, heat some oil over medium-high flame.
6. Dip a spoon into the hot oil to coat and then measure out 1 rounded tablespoon of the cornmeal batter into the pan. Cook the corn fritters until golden brown on both sides. Transfer into a plate lined with paper towels to drain excess oil.
7. Serve and enjoy.

Nutritional Information:
Energy - 260 kcal; Fat – 9.7 g; Carbs – 40.9 g; Protein – 7.1 g; Sodium – 186 mg

SOUTHERN COOKING

Crispy Chicken Fingers

Preparation Time: 12 minutes; **Total Time:** 30 minutes; **Yield:** 8 servings

Ingredients
2.2 lbs. (1 kg) chicken tenders, cut into 1-inch thick strips
1 ½ cups (180 g) all-purpose flour
1 tsp. (5 g) salt
1/2 tsp. (1 g) black pepper
1 large egg (60 g), beaten + 2 tablespoons (30 ml) water
canola oil, for frying

Method
1. In a large bowl, combine the pepper, salt, and flour.
2. Whisk together water and egg in another bowl.
3. Coat well all sides of the chicken with flour. Remove excess flour and dip in egg, then return in the flour. Let sit for about 5 minutes.
4. Meanwhile, heat oil in a deep frying pan over high heat. Cook chicken tenders in batches until golden brown, about 6 to 10 minutes.
5. Transfer into a paper towel-lined plate to absorb excess oil.
6. Serve and enjoy.

Nutritional Information:
Energy - 315 kcal; Fat – 14.9 g; Carbs – 12.1 g; Protein – 31.1 g; Sodium – 311 mg

Oven-Baked Chicken Meatballs

Preparation Time: 12 minutes; **Total Time:** 30 minutes; **Yield:** 6 servings

Ingredients
1 lb. (450 g) ground chicken breast
1/2 cup (60 g) breadcrumbs
2 Tbsp. (7 g) fresh rosemary, chopped
1/2 cup (60 g) cheddar cheese, grated
1/2 tsp. (1 g) garlic powder
1/2 tsp. (2.5 g) sea salt
1/2 tsp. (1 g) freshly ground black pepper
1 (60 g) large egg
cooking oil spray

Method
1. Preheat oven to 400°F (200°C).
2. In a large mixing bowl, combine ground chicken, breadcrumbs, rosemary, cheese, garlic powder, salt, pepper, and egg. Mix thoroughly.
3. Form the mixture into 2-inch meatballs using your hands. Place the meatballs into a lightly greased baking dish, leaving some space in between meatballs to cook evenly.
4. Bake for about 25 minutes, or until golden brown and cooked through.
5. Serve with dipping sauce and enjoy.

Nutritional Information:
Energy - 251 kcal; Fat – 14.4 g; Carbs – 7.6 g; Protein – 23.6 g; Sodium – 368 mg

SOUTHERN COOKING

Potato Fritters with Herbed Sour Cream

Preparation Time: 11 minutes; **Total Time:** 30 minutes; **Yield:** 8 servings

Ingredients
2.2 lbs. (1 kg) potatoes peeled grated
1 (110 g) onion, chopped
1 (60 g) large egg
1/2 cup (50 g) seasoned breadcrumbs
2 Tbsp. (7 g) fresh parsley, chopped
2 Tbsp. (7 g) scallions, chopped
salt and freshly ground black pepper

vegetable oil, for frying

Herbed Sour Cream Dipping Sauce:
1/2 cup (125 g) sour cream
2 Tbsp. (7 g) fresh chives, chopped
1 clove (3 g) garlic, minced
salt and freshly ground black pepper

Method
1. In a small bowl, mix together all ingredients for the dipping sauce then add pepper and salt. Set aside.
2. Combine the potatoes, shallots, egg, breadcrumbs, parsley, and scallions in a medium bowl then add pepper and salt. Mix well.
3. Over medium-high heat, heat oil in a non-stick pan.
4. Take about 2 tablespoons of mixture and roll. Do the same for the rest of the mixture then fry in batches until golden both sides are golden brown; press gently to flatten.
5. Drain excess oil by transferring into a plate lined with paper towels.
6. Serve with the prepared dipping sauce.

Nutritional Information:
Energy - 206 kcal; Fat – 10.8 g; Carbs – 24.3 g; Protein – 4.4 g; Sodium – 178 mg

Les Ilagan

SOUPS

Cream of Carrot and Pepper Soup

Preparation Time: 10 minutes; **Total Time:** 30 minutes; **Yield:** 4 servings

Ingredients
2.2 lbs. (1 kg) carrot thinly sliced
1 ½ cups (240 g) yellow onion, chopped
2 cups (500 ml) water
6 oz. (180 g) roasted red bell peppers

1 cup (250 ml) half and half cream
2 Tbsp. (30 ml) lemon juice
1/2 tsp. (2.5 g) salt
1/2 tsp. (1 g) ground black pepper

Method
1. Over medium-high flame, heat oil in a large saucepan. Add the carrot, onion, and water then simmer for 20 minutes while covered until carrots are tender. Cool slightly. Transfer to a heavy-duty blender. Add roasted bell peppers and blend on high speed until smooth.
2. Return soup to pan. Stir in half and half cream and lemon juice; cook until heated through then add pepper and salt to season it.
3. Divide among 4 serving bowls.
4. Serve and enjoy.

Nutritional Information:
Energy - 206 kcal; Fat – 7.1 g; Carbs – 32.3 g; Protein – 4.2 g; Sodium – 465 mg

Cream of Pumpkin Soup with Chili

Preparation Time: 10 minutes; **Total Time:** 30 minutes; **Yield:** 4 servings

Ingredients
1 Tbsp. (15 ml) vegetable oil
2.2 lbs. (1 kg) pumpkin
1 large carrot
4 cups (1 L) of vegetable stock or chicken stock
1 red long chili, seeds removed
1 tsp. (5 g) ginger, grated
6 oz. (180 ml) coconut cream
salt and freshly ground black pepper

Method
1. Peel carrot and pumpkin. Cut into small pieces.
2. Over medium-high flame, heat oil in a large saucepan; then add the pumpkin and carrot. Cook, stirring, for 3 minutes or until lightly browned.
3. Add the stock along with ginger and chopped chili and allow to simmer for 20 minutes or until vegetables are fork tender.
4. Remove from heat and cool slightly then using a stick blender, blend the soup.
5. Add the coconut cream and heat until the soup comes back up to the boil then add pepper and salt.
6. Serve and enjoy.

Nutritional Information:
Energy - 211 kcal; Fat – 10.2 g; Carbs – 23.3 g; Protein – 2.2 g; Sodium – 235 mg

Hearty Broccoli and Corn Soup

Preparation Time: 12 minutes; **Total Time:** 30 minutes; **Yield:** 6 servings

Ingredients

2 Tbsp. (30 g) butter
1 medium (110 g) onion, chopped
2 cloves garlic, chopped
8 oz. (250 g) beef sausage, chopped
10 oz. (300 g) frozen corn, thawed
2 medium potatoes, diced

2 (60 g) stalks celery, diced
2 cups (500 ml) beef stock
2 cups (500 ml) water
1 cup (250 ml) half & half cream
2 Tbsp. (7 g) fresh coriander, chopped
salt and freshly ground black pepper

Method

1. Over medium flame, heat butter in a large saucepan. Stir-fry onion and garlic for 1 minute or until aromatic.
2. Stir in sausage and cook for 5 minutes.
3. Add the corn, potatoes, celery, and chicken stock. Bring to a boil. Reduce heat and simmer covered with lid for 25 minutes.
4. Add the milk and coriander, cook further 5 minutes, stirring frequently. Season to taste. Remove from heat.
5. Ladle in serving bowls. Garnish with coriander, if desired.
6. Serve and enjoy.

Nutritional Information:

Energy - 192 kcal; Fat – 10.1 g; Carbs – 24.7 g; Protein – 5.0 g; Sodium – 544 mg

Pumpkin and Corn Soup

Preparation Time: 12 minutes; **Total Time:** 30 minutes; **Yield:** 6 servings

Ingredients

2 Tbsp. (30 ml) olive oil
1 medium (110 g) red onion, chopped
2 cloves (6 g) garlic, minced
1 lb. (450 g) broccoli florets, cut into small pieces
1 medium (60 g) carrot, diced

16 oz. (480 g) canned cream-style corn
2 cups (500 ml) chicken stock
250 ml (4.23 oz.) half & half cream
1/4 cup (15 g) flat-leaf parsley, chopped
salt and freshly ground black pepper

Method

1. In a large saucepan, stir-fry onion and garlic for 3 minutes or until fragrant over medium-high heat.
2. Add broccoli, carrot, corn, stock, and water. Reduce heat. Cover and simmer for 15 minutes.
3. Add the cream and parsley. Cook further 5 minutes, then season to taste.
4. Ladle in individual soup bowls.
5. Serve and enjoy.

Nutritional Information:

Energy - 198 kcal; Fat – 12.7 g; Carbs – 21.7 g; Protein – 5.1 g; Sodium – 424 mg

Les Ilagan

Pumpkin Soup with Sour Cream

Preparation Time: 12 minutes; **Total Time:** 30 minutes; **Yield:** 6 servings

Ingredients
2 Tbsp. (30 ml) olive oil
2 pcs. (80 g) shallot, sliced
2 (6 g) cloves garlic, minced
1 lb. (450 g) pumpkin, diced
8 oz. (250 g) frozen corn, thawed
3 cups (750 ml) chicken stock, reduced sodium
1 cup (250 ml) half & half cream
2 Tbsp. (15 g) fresh parsley, chopped
salt and freshly ground black pepper
yogurt, to serve

Method
1. In a large saucepan, stir-fry shallots and garlic for 2-3 minutes or until aromatic over medium-high heat.
2. Add the pumpkin, corn, stock, and water. Reduce heat. Cover with lid and simmer for 25 minutes, stirring occasionally. Remove from heat.
3. Transfer soup in a food processor or blender. Pulse a few times to coarsely chop the pumpkin and the corn. Return to saucepan, add the cream and parsley. Cook over medium-high heat for 5 minutes then add pepper and salt.
4. Ladle in serving bowls, then add a spoonful of yogurt on top.
5. Serve and enjoy.

Nutritional Information:
Energy - 208 kcal; Fat – 13.2 g; Carbs – 22.7 g; Protein – 3.5 g; Sodium – 413 mg

SOUTHERN COOKING

MAINS

Classic Shrimp Po Boy

Preparation Time: 20 minutes; **Total Time:** 40 minutes; **Yield:** 4 servings

Ingredients
1/2 tsp. (1 g) cayenne pepper
1/2 tsp. (1 g) garlic powder
1/2 tsp. (1 g) paprika
1/2 tsp. (2.5 g) Kosher salt
1/2 tsp. (1 g) sage (dried)
1/2 tsp. (1 g) thyme (dried)
1/2 tsp. (1 g) onion powder
1/2 tsp. (1 g) freshly ground black pepper
1 lb. (450 g) medium shrimp (peeled and deveined)
1 cup (250 ml) buttermilk

1 cup (125 g) all-purpose flour
1 cup (175 g) fine cornmeal
6 (8-inch) French rolls (split)
vegetable oil for frying

To Serve:
light mayonnaise
Romaine lettuce
sliced tomatoes
dill pickles
hot pepper sauce (optional)

Method
1. Mix together the seasonings and dried herbs in a small bowl.
2. Heat enough oil in a deep skillet over medium-high heat.
3. In a medium bowl, toss shrimps and 2 tablespoons seasoning mix.
4. In a small bowl, place buttermilk then in another bowl, mix flour and cornmeal.
5. Dip each seasoned shrimp in buttermilk, coat in the flour mixture. Repeat with remaining shrimps. Deep fry in batches until golden brown, stirring occasionally and put in a platter lined with paper towels to drain excess oil.
6. Open French rolls. Spread each with 1 ½ Tbsp. mayonnaise. Add the lettuce, tomato slices, and pickles. Top with shrimps. Serve with hot sauce, if desired.

Nutritional Information:
Energy - 352 kcal; Fat – 12.5 g; Carbs – 37.5 g; Protein – 22.9 g; Sodium - 643 mg

Les Ilagan

Roast Beef with Pepper and Rosemary

Preparation Time: 15 minutes; **Total Time:** 45 minutes; **Yield:** 8 servings

Ingredients
1 Tbsp. (10 g) garlic, chopped
1 tsp. (5 g) Kosher salt, divided
2 Tbsp. (30 ml) olive oil
3 lbs. (1.4 kg) beef tri-tip roast, trimmed
3 Tbsp. (7 g) fresh rosemary, chopped
1 Tbsp. (6 g) whole black peppercorns, coarsely ground
1 Tbsp. (6 g) whole white peppercorns, coarsely ground
2 Tbsp. (30 g) butter

Method
1. Grind garlic and a pinch of kosher salt using mortar and pestle until a paste is formed. Add olive oil into garlic mixture.
2. In a baking dish, brush beef with prepared garlic paste on both sides of the roast. Season with kosher salt.
3. Combine peppercorns and rosemary in a small bowl.
4. Heat butter in a large ovenproof pan. Turn off heat then coat beef (both sides).
5. Roll the beef onto the peppercorn-rosemary mixture and coat generously.
6. Preheat oven to 450°F (225°C).
7. Roast meat in the pan in the preheated oven for about 15 minutes. Remove meat from the oven and turn to cook the other side.
8. Reduce oven temperature to 350°F (175°C). Cook further 15 minutes or until pepper crust is lightly toasted.
9. Place roast beef to a platter and cover loosely with aluminum foil. Cool slightly for 10-15 minutes before cutting across the grain.
10. Serve slices on individual plates drizzled with pan sauce.

Nutritional Information:
Energy - 296 kcal; Fat – 14.2 g; Carbs – 2.9 g; Protein – 38.1 g; Sodium - 395 mg

SOUTHERN COOKING

Crab Cakes in Lemony Tartar Sauce with Dill

Preparation Time: 12 minutes; **Total Time:** 48 minutes; **Yield:** 6 servings

Ingredients
16 oz. (450 g) crabmeat, shredded
3/4 cup (75 g) breadcrumbs, dry
1 large (60 g) egg, lightly beaten
1/4 cup (15 g) scallions, finely chopped
2 Tbsp. (15 g) all-purpose flour
2 Tbsp. (30 ml) lemon juice
1/2 tsp. (2.5 g) lemon zest, finely grated
1 tsp. (2 g) garlic powder
1/2 tsp. (2.5 g) Kosher salt
1/2 tsp. (1 g) freshly ground black pepper

2 Tbsp. (30 ml) vegetable oil
lemon wedges (to serve)

Lemony Tartar Sauce with Dill:
2/3 cup (165 g) light mayonnaise
2 Tbsp. (30 ml) lemon juice
1 Tbsp. (7 g) fresh dill weed, minced
1 clove (3 g) garlic, minced
salt and freshly ground black pepper

Method
1. Mix well all ingredients except oil, lemon wedges, and sauce ingredients. Form into 12 round patties and refrigerate for 20 minutes to firm up.
2. Meanwhile, mix all sauce ingredients. Keep refrigerated until needed.
3. Over medium-high flame, heat oil in a large pan; then fry the crab cakes until crisp and golden. Drain into a serving platter lined with paper towels to drain.
4. Serve with prepared sauce and lemon wedges then you may garnish with fresh dill weed if you want.

Nutritional Information:
Energy - 295 kcal; Fat – 15.1 g; Carbs – 30.3 g; Protein – 9.2 g; Sodium - 895 mg

Cajun Spiced Grilled Chicken Breast with Honey

Preparation Time: 15 minutes; **Total Time:** 1 hour 30 minutes; **Yield:** 4 servings

Ingredients
!/4 cup (60 ml) olive oil
1 Tbsp. (6 g) Cajun seasoning
2 Tbsp. (40 ml) honey
2 tsp. (4 g) lemon pepper, ground
1 tsp. (2 g) garlic powder
1/2 tsp. (2.5 g) Kosher salt
4 (5 oz. or 150 g) chicken breast – boneless, skinless (pounded to ½-inch thickness)
cooking oil spray

Method
1. Whisk together the oil, Cajun seasoning, honey, garlic powder, and lemon pepper in a shallow dish.
2. Add the chicken breasts and turn to coat all sides with the mixture. Keep in the fridge covered for a minimum of 1 hour.
3. Preheat the grill to high. Lightly oil the grill grate with oil spray.
4. Drain the chicken breasts and discard marinade.
5. Grill chicken for 7 to 8 minutes on each side, or until juices run clear. Transfer to a serving dish.
6. Serve immediately and enjoy.

Nutritional Information:
Energy - 298 kcal; Fat – 14.1 g; Carbs – 9.8 g; Protein – 33.0 g; Sodium - 257 mg

SOUTHERN COOKING

Country Style Crispy Fried Chicken with Buttermilk

Preparation Time: 10 minutes; **Total Time:** 2 hours 30 minutes; **Yield:** 8 servings

Ingredients
1 ½ cups (375 ml) buttermilk
2 Tbsp. (30 g) Dijon mustard
1 tsp. (2 g) cayenne pepper
1 tsp. (5 g) Kosher salt
1 tsp. (2 g) ground black pepper
1 whole chicken, cut into 8 pieces

1 ½ cups (185 g) all-purpose flour
2 tsp. (8 g) baking powder
2 tsp. (4 g) garlic powder
2 tsp. (4 g) onion powder
cooking oil

Method
1. Whisk together buttermilk, mustard, cayenne pepper, Kosher salt, and pepper in a non-reactive shallow dish.
2. Add the chicken pieces, turn to coat all sides with the marinade. Keep in the fridge marinated and covered in plastic wrap for a minimum of 2 hours.
3. Mix together the all-purpose flour, baking powder, onion powder, and garlic powder in a resealable plastic bag. Shake to mix thoroughly.
4. Put 1 marinated chicken at a time into the bag with seasoning mix. Shake to coat the chicken well.
5. Over medium-high flame, heat oil in a large saucepan; then fry the chicken pieces in batches until golden brown and juices run clear, turning a few times to cook evenly.
6. Transfer to a serving dish.
7. Serve and enjoy.

Nutritional Information:
Energy - 346 kcal; Fat – 13.5 g; Carbs – 15.3 g; Protein – 39.2 g; Sodium - 356 mg

Pepper Crusted Cod Fillet with Paprika

Preparation Time: 10 minutes; **Total Time:** 20 minutes; **Yield:** 4 servings

Ingredients
1/4 cup (25 g) black pepper (coarsely ground)
1 tsp. (2 g) sweet paprika
1 tsp. (2 g) garlic powder

4 (5 oz. or 150 g) cod fillets
2 Tbsp. (30 ml) olive oil
cooking oil spray

Method
1. Preheat grill or griddle to high and spray with oil.
2. Mix together pepper, paprika, and garlic powder in a shallow dish.
3. Drizzle cod fillets with 2 tablespoons olive oil and rub to coat all sides.
4. Press into the pepper mixture, turn to coat the other side. Grill cod fillets until it flakes easily with a fork, about 10-12 minutes.
5. Transfer to a serving dish.
6. Serve and enjoy.

Nutritional Information:
Energy - 281 kcal; Fat – 16.1 g; Carbs – 2.2 g; Protein – 31.4 g; Sodium - 305 mg

Southern Fried Chicken Wings in Spicy BBQ Sauce

Preparation Time: 15 minutes; **Total Time:** 35 minutes; **Yield:** 8 servings

Ingredients
2.2 lbs. (1 kg) chicken wings
salt and freshly ground black pepper
1 cup (125 g) all-purpose flour
1 tsp. (2 g) cumin (ground)
1 tsp. (2 g) paprika
1/2 tsp. (1 g) garlic powder
1/2 tsp. (1 g) freshly ground black pepper
vegetable oil

2/3 cup (165 g) ketchup
1/4 cup (55 g) brown sugar
2 Tbsp. (30 ml) white wine vinegar
1 tsp. (5 ml) soy sauce
1 tsp. (2 g) garlic powder
1/2 tsp. (1 g) cayenne pepper
1/2 tsp. (1 g) hot paprika
1/2 tsp. (1 g) black pepper
1 tsp. (2.5 g) cornstarch
1/4 cup (60 ml) water

Spicy Barbecue Sauce:

Method
1. Bring barbecue sauce ingredients to a boil except for cornstarch and water. Dilute cornstarch in water then add into barbecue sauce mixture. Cook until thickened about 5 minutes before transferring to a small bowl. Set aside until needed.
2. Prepare chicken pieces by seasoning with pepper and salt.
3. In a shallow bowl, mix flour, cumin, paprika, and garlic powder. Roll chicken wings one at a time to coat all sides.
4. Over medium-high flame, heat oil in a large pan; then cook chicken until golden brown for 20 minutes, turning half-way through to cook evenly.
5. Transfer to a large plate with paper towels to drain and serve with the prepared spicy barbecue sauce.

Nutritional Information:
Energy - 376 kcal; Fat – 16.2 g; Carbs – 22.7 g; Protein – 35.3 g; Sodium - 360 mg

Spiced Chicken Drumstick with Thyme

Preparation Time: 15 minutes; **Total Time:** 30 minutes; **Yield:** 6 servings

Ingredients
1 tsp. (2 g) paprika
1 tsp. (5 g) Kosher salt
1 tsp. (2 g) garlic powder
1 tsp. (2 g) onion powder
1 tsp. (2 g) thyme (dried)

1 tsp. (2 g) cayenne pepper, ground
1 tsp. (2 g) freshly ground black pepper
4 pcs. chicken leg or drumstick
cooking oil spray

Method
1. Mix together the paprika, salt, garlic powder, onion powder, thyme, cayenne pepper, and black pepper in a medium bowl.
2. Rub chicken legs with the spice mixture, coating evenly.
3. Preheat grill to medium-high heat. Lightly spray the grill grate with oil.
4. Grill chicken legs for 6 to 8 minutes on each side, or until juices run clear.
5. Transfer to a serving dish.
6. Serve immediately and enjoy.

Nutritional Information:
Energy - 224 kcal; Fat – 12.5 g; Carbs – 1.1 g; Protein – 28.2 g; Sodium - 376 mg

Meat Potato and Cheese Casserole

Preparation Time: 10 minutes; **Total Time:** 50 minutes; **Yield:** 8 servings

Ingredients
4 cups (1000 g) leftover mashed potatoes
2 Tbsp. (30 ml) olive oil
1 medium (110 g) onion, chopped
1 tsp. (3 g) garlic, minced
1 ½ lb. (675 g) ground beef sirloin
1 (24 oz.) jar pasta sauce

1/2 tsp. (2 g) red pepper flakes
1/2 tsp. (1 g) thyme (dried)
1/2 cup (60 g) mozzarella cheese, shredded
1/4 cup (60 g) cheddar cheese, grated
salt and freshly ground black pepper

Method
1. Preheat the oven to 350°F (175°C).
2. Over medium-high flame, heat oil in a large pan; then stir-fry onion and garlic for 3 minutes.
3. Add the ground beef and cook for 5-7 minutes or until browned.
4. Stir in pasta sauce, red pepper flakes, and thyme. Cook for another 15 minutes then add pepper and salt to season it. Remove from heat.
5. Pour beef mixture into an 8x8-inch casserole dish. Top with mashed potatoes. Sprinkle mozzarella cheese and cheddar cheese over the dish.
6. Bake in the preheated oven until the mozzarella cheese melts and the potatoes are heated through, about 10-15 minutes.
7. Serve and enjoy.

Nutritional Information:
Energy - 371 kcal; Fat – 14.3 g; Carbs – 33.2 g; Protein – 32.4 g; Sodium - 587 mg

Baked Turkey Meatballs with Spicy Yogurt Dip

Preparation Time: 25 minutes; **Total Time:** 50 minutes; **Yield:** 6 servings

Ingredients
2.2 lbs. (1 kg) turkey breast, ground
1 cup (100 g) breadcrumbs
1 large (60 g) egg
1/4 cup (15 g) fresh coriander, chopped
1/2 tsp. (1 g) garlic powder
1/2 tsp. (2.5 g) Kosher salt
1/2 tsp. (1 g) freshly ground black pepper
Cooking oil spray

Spicy Yogurt Dip:
1 cup (250 g) plain yogurt
1 Tbsp. (15 ml) lemon juice
1/2 tsp. (1 g) chipotle chili powder
1/2 tsp. (1 g) paprika (ground)
salt and freshly ground black pepper

Method
1. Preheat oven to 400°F (200°C).
2. In a small bowl, mix together yogurt, lemon juice, chipotle, and paprika then keep it in the fridge until needed.
3. Combine turkey, breadcrumbs, egg, fresh coriander, garlic powder, salt, and black pepper. Mix well.
4. Take about 2 tablespoons of turkey mixture and form into a ball. Repeat with the remaining mixture and arrange on a lightly greased baking dish. Spray turkey meatballs with oil.
5. Bake in the oven for 20-25 minutes or until browned and cooked through.
6. Serve the turkey meatballs on a serving dish with spicy yogurt dip on the side.

Nutritional Information:
Energy - 205 kcal; Fat – 4.3 g; Carbs – 17.0 g; Protein – 24.9 g; Sodium - 430 mg

Honey Mustard Chicken Roast

Preparation Time: 15 minutes; **Total Time:** 1 hour; **Yield:** 8 servings

Ingredients

1 whole chicken
salt and pepper to taste
1/2 cup (170 ml) honey
1/4 cup (60 g) Dijon mustard
2 Tbsp. (30 g) regular mustard
2 Tbsp. (30 ml) lemon juice

1 tsp. (2 g) dried rosemary
1/2 tsp. (1 g) dried parsley
1/2 tsp. (1 g) paprika
2 cloves (6 g) garlic, minced
cooking oil spray

Method

1. Preheat oven to 350°F (175°C). Lightly grease a 9x13-inch baking dish with oil spray.
2. Season chicken with pepper and salt then set aside.
3. In a small bowl, combine the honey, Dijon mustard, regular mustard, lemon juice, rosemary, parsley, paprika, and garlic. Mix well. Pour half of the mixture over the chicken and coat all sides by the brushing mixture into the chicken.
4. Bake in the preheated oven. Turn the chicken after 15 minutes then brush with the remaining honey mustard mixture. Bake for the same duration on the other side. Bake further for 15 minutes, or until chicken is golden brown and juices run clear. Remove from heat and let stand for 10 minutes to cool before slicing.
5. Serve and enjoy.

Nutritional Information:

Energy - 313 kcal; Fat – 11.0 g; Carbs – 13.5 g; Protein – 37.3 g; Sodium - 316 mg

Les Ilagan

Savory Shrimp and Grits with Thyme

Preparation Time: 10 minutes; **Total Time:** 28 minutes; **Yield:** 6 servings

Ingredients
3 cups (750 ml) water
1/2 tsp. (2.5 g) Kosher salt
1 cup (175 g) grits quick cooking
1 (7 oz. or 200 g) package garlic cheese spread
2 Tbsp. (30 g) butter
2 tsp. (10 ml) olive oil
1 ½ lb. (675 g) fresh shrimp, peeled and deveined
2 Tbsp. (30 g) tomato sauce
2 Tbsp. (30 g) ketchup
1 Tbsp. (3.5 g) fresh thyme, chopped
salt and freshly ground black pepper

Method
1. In a saucepan, bring the water and Kosher salt to a boil over high heat. Stir in quick grits and lower heat to medium. Simmer for 5 minutes, stirring often. Remove from heat.
2. Add the garlic cheese spread and mix until well combined. Let stand for 3-4 minutes.
3. In a skillet or non-stick pan, heat butter and olive oil over medium heat. Stir-fry the shrimp for 2 minutes.
4. Add the tomato sauce, ketchup, and thyme. Cook further 5 minutes then remove from heat add pepper and salt.
5. Spread the cheese grits on warm serving plates. Top with savory shrimp mixture.
6. Serve immediately and enjoy.

Nutritional Information:
Energy - 291 kcal; Fat – 14.1 g; Carbs – 6.6 g; Protein – 33.7 g; Sodium - 568 mg

Tasty Buffalo Wings

Preparation Time: 10 minutes; **Total Time:** 25 minutes; **Yield:** 8 servings

Ingredients

- 2.2 lbs. (1 kg) chicken wings
- 1/2 cup (125 g) cold unsalted butter
- 1/2 cup (125 ml) hot pepper sauce
- 2 Tbsp. (30 g) ketchup
- 1 Tbsp. (15 ml) white vinegar
- 1 tsp. (5 ml) Worcestershire sauce
- 1/2 tsp. (1 g) garlic powder
- 1/2 tsp. (1 g) cayenne pepper
- salt and freshly ground black pepper
- cooking oil

Method

1. Lightly season chicken wings with salt and pepper. Set aside.
2. Heat a generous amount of oil in a large skillet or deep fryer over medium-high heat. Deep fry chicken wings in oil until golden brown, about 10-12 minutes. Remove chicken and place into a platter lined with paper towels to drain.
3. Over medium-high heat, heat oil in a large pan; then stir in the hot pepper sauce, ketchup, white vinegar, Worcestershire sauce, garlic powder, and cayenne pepper. Mix well then add pepper and salt.
4. Add the fried chicken wings to sauce and cook further 10 minutes, stirring often.
5. Serve immediately and enjoy.

Nutritional Information:

Energy - 332 kcal; Fat – 20.2 g; Carbs – 1.1 g; Protein – 33.4 g; Sodium - 264 mg

Baked Honey-Mustard Drumsticks

Preparation Time: 10 minutes; **Total Time:** 30 minutes; **Yield:** 10 servings

Ingredients

- 1/4 cup (80 ml) pure honey
- 2 Tbsp. (30 g) Dijon mustard
- 1 Tbsp. (15 ml) olive oil
- 1 tsp. (5 g) wholegrain mustard
- 1 tsp. (2 g) dried mixed herbs
- 1 tsp. (3 g) garlic, minced
- 8 chicken drumsticks (about 1 kg)
- 1 medium (200 g) zucchini, thinly sliced crosswise
- 1 medium (60 g) carrot, thinly sliced crosswise
- 1 medium (110 g) onion, thinly sliced crosswise
- 1 leek, thinly sliced diagonally
- cooking oil spray

Method

1. Preheat your oven to 400°F (200°C).
2. Mix together honey, Dijon mustard, wholegrain mustard, mixed herbs, and garlic in a bowl.
3. Place chicken in a single layer, in a glass baking dish. Then, pour the honey mixture. Turn to coat all sides.
4. Add the vegetables on the sides of the chicken. Spray with oil then add pepper and salt to season it.
5. Bake in the preheated oven to 45 to 50 minutes or until chicken is cooked through and vegetables are tender, turning halfway through cooking time.
6. Serve and enjoy.

Nutritional Information:

Energy - 259 kcal; Fat – 5.8 g; Carbs – 13.5 g; Protein – 37.1 g; Sodium – 134 mg

SOUTHERN COOKING

Beef and Pumpkin Stew

Preparation Time: 12 minutes; **Total Time:** 30 minutes; **Yield:** 8 servings

Ingredients
2 Tbsp. (30 ml) olive oil
3 lbs. (1.4 kg) beef short ribs
2 (110 g) red onions, chopped
1 tsp. (2 g) garlic, minced
1 tsp. (2 g) dried oregano
1 tsp. (2 g) dried thyme
1 bay leaf
3 cups (750 ml) beef broth
1 cup (250 g) tomato sauce
¼ cup (60 g) tomato paste
3 (60 g) stalks celery, diced
2 (200 g) potatoes, peeled and cubed
1 medium (60 g) carrot, peeled and cubed
1 lb. (450 g) pumpkin, peeled and cubed
kosher salt and freshly ground black pepper

Method
1. Over medium-high heat, heat oil in a large pan; then stir-fry onions and garlic followed by the meat. Brown both sides.
2. Next, add in oregano, thyme, bay leaf, broth, tomato sauce, and tomato paste; bring to a boil. Reduce heat, cook covered for 2 hours or until almost tender.
3. Add the vegetables; simmer until the vegetables are tender then add pepper and salt.
4. Serve and enjoy.

Nutritional Information:
Energy - 275 kcal; Fat – 9.2 g; Carbs – 16.5 g; Protein – 31.2 g; Sodium – 438 mg

Beef Stew with Polenta

Preparation Time: 10 minutes; **Total Time:** 30 minutes; **Yield:** 4 servings

Ingredients
1/4 cup (30 g) plain flour
2.2 lbs. (1 kg.) beef chuck roast, cubed
2 Tbsp. (30 ml) olive oil
1 medium (110 g) onion, chopped
2 garlic (3 g) cloves, minced
4 (125 g) tomatoes, sliced lengthwise
1 cup (150 g) button mushrooms, sliced
2 (60 g) stalks celery, diced
8 (10 g) pitted olives
2 cups (500 ml) beef stock
¼ cup (60 ml) tomato paste
2 Tbsp. (30 ml) apple cider vinegar
1/2 cup (30 g) fresh basil leaves, chopped
1 ½ Tbsp. (10 g) rosemary leaves, chopped
kosher salt and ground black pepper

For the Polenta:
2 cups (500 ml) whole milk
1 cup (160 g) polenta
1 Tbsp. (15 g) unsalted butter
¼ cup (25 g) parmesan cheese, grated finely

Method
1. In a resealable bag, zip and shake beef and flour to coat. Over medium-high flame, heat oil in a large pan; then cook beef until browned for 7 minutes. Transfer to a plate.
2. In the same pan, stir-fry onion, garlic, carrot and celery to the same pan, about 3 minutes. Return beef and juices to pan.
3. Add parsnip, rosemary, stock, tomato paste, and vinegar. Boil then reduce heat to low. Simmer, covered, for 1 hour. Add basil and rosemary. Stir occasionally and cook until tender for 30 minutes.
4. For the polenta, boil milk and 2 cups cold water in a saucepan over medium-high heat then gradually stir in polenta. Cook over low heat. Stir until thick.
5. Stir in parmesan cheese then serve beef stew on top of polenta.

Nutritional Information:
Energy - 389 kcal; Fat – 15.0 g; Carbs – 28.2 g; Protein – 35.3 g; Sodium – 384 mg

SOUTHERN COOKING

Breaded Chicken Cutlets

Preparation Time: 12 minutes; **Total Time:** 30 minutes; **Yield:** 6 servings

Ingredients
4 (5 oz. or 150 g) boneless, skinless chicken breasts
1 cup (100 g) seasoned dry breadcrumbs
1 tsp. (2 g) dried rosemary
1/2 tsp. (2.5 g) lemon, zested
1/2 tsp. (2.5 g) kosher salt
1/4 tsp. (1.5 g) ground black pepper
1/2 cup (60 g) all-purpose flour
2 (60 g) whole eggs
vegetable oil, for frying

Method
1. Place one chicken breast between two sheets of plastic wrap then pound it to ¼-inch thick using a flat meat mallet. Repeat with remaining chicken breasts.
2. In a large shallow bowl, combine breadcrumbs, rosemary, lemon zest, salt, and black pepper.
3. In a separate shallow bowl, crack eggs and beat to combine then put the flour in another shallow bowl.
4. Preheat your oven to 400°F (200°C).
5. Dredge a chicken piece in flour, turning to coat all sides. Dip into the beaten eggs, coating it fully. Then, place it onto the breadcrumb mixture and coat well. Place chicken on a large plate. Repeat with the remaining chicken pieces.
6. Put a wire rack over a baking sheet.
7. Over medium-high heat and in a large pan, heat enough oil then cook chicken through until both sides are golden brown.
8. Drain the excess oil by transferring to a plate lined with paper towels.
9. Serve and enjoy.

Nutritional Information:
Energy - 404 kcal; Fat – 16.4 g; Carbs – 22.0 g; Protein – 39.3 g; Sodium – 389 mg

Breaded Turkey Breast with Rosemary

Preparation Time: 12 minutes; **Total Time:** 30 minutes; **Yield:** 6 servings

Ingredients
1 ½ lb. (675 g) boneless, skinless turkey breast
½ cup (120 g) light mayonnaise
¼ cup (60 ml) Dijon mustard
1 ½ cups (150 g) panko breadcrumbs
½ cup (60 g) grated Parmesan cheese
2 Tbsp. (7 g) fresh rosemary, chopped

Method
1. Preheat oven to 450°F (225°C).
2. Cut the turkey breast into four equal portions and pound to 1/4-inch thickness.
3. Whisk together mayonnaise and mustard.
4. In a shallow bowl, mix the breadcrumbs, Parmesan, and rosemary.
5. Dip each turkey piece in mayonnaise mixture, then coat with breadcrumb mixture.
6. Place the breaded turkey cutlets on a lined baking sheet.
7. Bake in the preheated oven for 15 minutes, or until just cooked through and golden brown.
8. Serve immediately.

Nutritional Information:
Energy - 339 kcal; Fat – 14.9 g; Carbs – 9.0 g; Protein – 31.5 g; Sodium – 402 mg

Broccoli and Cheese Quiche

Preparation Time: 12 minutes; **Total Time:** 30 minutes; **Yield:** 6 servings

Ingredients
2 Tbsp. (30 g) butter
1 medium (110 g) onion, chopped
1 tsp. (5 g) garlic, minced
2 cups (350 g) broccoli head, chopped
1 (9-inch or 22 cm) unbaked pie crust
2 Tbsp. (10 g) Parmesan cheese

4 (60 g) whole eggs, well beaten
1 ½ cups (375 ml) skim milk
1 tsp. (5 g) kosher salt
1/2 tsp. (1 g) freshly ground black pepper
1 cup (125 g) shredded mozzarella cheese
1 Tbsp. (15 ml) butter, melted

Method
1. Preheat oven to 350°F (180°C).
2. In a pie plate, place the crust.
3. Over medium-low flame, heat butter in a large pan. Stir-fry onions, garlic, and broccoli until the vegetables are soft. Spoon vegetables into the crust and sprinkle with parmesan.
4. Combine eggs and milk then add pepper and salt. Pour over vegetables and cheese.
5. Bake in preheated oven for 30 minutes. Sprinkle with mozzarella and continue baking for another 15 minutes or until center has set. Cool slightly before cutting.
6. Serve and enjoy.

Nutritional Information:
Energy - 307 kcal; Fat – 20.0 g; Carbs – 21.8 g; Protein – 10.6 g; Sodium – 413 mg

Les Ilagan

Cajun Shrimps with Herbs

Preparation Time: 12 minutes; **Total Time:** 30 minutes; **Yield:** 6 servings

Ingredients

1 tsp. Creole seasoning
1 lb. (450 g) large shrimp, peeled then deveined
4 oz. (120 g) unsalted butter, divided
2 tsp. (6 g) garlic, minced
2 Tbsp. (7 g) fresh parsley, chopped
1 tsp. (1 g) fresh sage, chopped
1 tsp. (1 g) fresh oregano, chopped
1/2 tsp. (1 g) paprika
Juice of ½ lemon
1/2 cup (125 ml) chicken stock
kosher salt and freshly ground black pepper

Method
1. Season the shrimp with creole seasoning.
2. Heat about 2 tablespoons of butter in a large pan over medium heat.
3. Stir-fry shrimp for about 3 to 5 minutes. Set aside.
4. Add remaining butter to the pan, once heated add the garlic; cook, stirring for about 1 to 2 minutes or until fragrant.
5. Stir in sage, oregano, paprika, lemon juice, and chicken stock; bring to a boil. Simmer for about 2 to 3 minutes.
6. Return the shrimp in the pan. Season to taste.
7. Serve immediately.

Nutritional Information:
Energy - 229 kcal; Fat – 16.7 g; Carbs – 1.8 g; Protein – 17.6 g; Sodium – 294 mg

Marinated Shrimps with Herbs

Preparation Time: 10 minutes; **Total Time:** 30 minutes; **Yield:** 4 servings

Ingredients

¼ cup (60 ml) olive oil
2 Tbsp. (30 ml) fresh lemon juice
2 Tbsp. (30 g) brown sugar, packed
2 Tbsp. (7 g) fresh mixed herbs, chopped
2.2 lbs. (1 kg) large shrimp, peeled then deveined

2 Tbsp. (20 g) garlic, minced
2 tsp. (4 g) smoked paprika
1/2 tsp. (1 g) ground black pepper
1/4 cup (15 g) fresh parsley, chopped

Method

1. Combine the oil, lemon juice, brown sugar, mixed herbs, garlic, paprika, and pepper in a large non-reactive bowl.
2. Toss in shrimp then set aside for at least 30 minutes.
3. Heat grill or griddle to high.
4. Cook the shrimps for 3-4 minutes on each side, or until just cooked.
5. Transfer to a serving dish. Sprinkle with chopped parsley.
6. Serve immediately.

Nutritional Information:

Energy - 204 kcal; Fat – 8.3 g; Carbs – 5.2 g; Protein – 26.1 g; Sodium – 280 mg

Les Ilagan

New Orleans Shrimp and Grits

Preparation Time: 12 minutes; **Total Time:** 30 minutes; **Yield:** 6 servings

Ingredients
For the Grits:
3 ½ cups (750 ml) water
3/4 cup (130 g) grits
1/4 tsp. (1.5) salt
4 oz. (120 g) cheddar cheese, grated
3 Tbsp. (45 g) butter

For the Shrimp:
2 Tbsp. (30 g) butter
1/2 cup (80 g) onion, chopped
2 cloves (6 g) garlic, minced

1 cup (250 g) canned diced tomatoes + juice
1/2 tsp. (1 g) dried thyme
1 Tbsp. (7 g) flour
1 lb. (450 g) med. raw shrimp, shelled
1 cup (250 ml) shrimp stock
1 Tbsp. (15 g) tomato paste
1/2 cup (125 ml) heavy cream
2 tsp. (10 ml) Worcestershire sauce
1 tsp. (5 ml) Tabasco
2 Tbsp. (15 g) fresh scallions, chopped
salt and freshly ground black pepper

Method
1. For the grits, boil water. Mix in grits. Cook covered until tender and all liquid is absorbed over low heat for 20 minutes. Remove from heat. Stir in salt, cheddar cheese, and butter. Keep warm.
2. Heat butter in a large skillet over medium flame. Stir-fry the onion and garlic until softened, about 3 minutes. Add tomatoes with juice and thyme; cook for 3 minutes. Add the flour and mix well.
3. Add shrimp; stir until pinkish, about 2 minutes. Add shrimp stock and cook for 3 minutes more then stir in tomato paste until blended.
4. Stir in cream, Worcestershire and Tabasco. Heat thoroughly, but don't boil. Add pepper and salt. Place a portion of cooked grits in the center of individual plates and spoon shrimp over. Sprinkle with chopped scallions.

Nutritional Information:
Energy - 481 kcal; Fat – 31.7 g; Carbs – 13.6 g; Protein – 34.9 g; Sodium – 616 mg

Garlic Lime Shrimp with Paprika

Preparation Time: 12 minutes; **Total Time:** 30 minutes; **Yield:** 8 servings

Ingredients
1 lb. (450 g) shrimp, peeled and deveined
2 Tbsp. (30 ml) vegetable oil, divided
1/2 tsp. (2.5 g) kosher salt
1/2 tsp. (1 g) freshly ground black pepper
pinch of sugar
2 Tbsp. (7 g) cilantro, chopped
juice of one lime
paprika to taste

Method
1. Pat dry shrimp with paper towels.
2. In a medium bowl, add the shrimp, salt, pepper, and sugar. Toss to coat.
3. Over medium-high heat, heat oil in a large pan; then cook shrimp for 3 minutes.
4. Add the juice of 1 lime. Sprinkle with paprika and cilantro. Mix well and cook for another 2 minutes while covered.
5. Transfer to a serving dish.
6. Serve hot.

Nutritional Information:
Energy - 202 kcal; Fat – 9.0 g; Carbs – 3.7 g; Protein – 26.0 g; Sodium – 556 mg

Grilled Chicken Drumstick and Corn

Preparation Time: 10 minutes; **Total Time:** 30 minutes; **Yield:** 4 servings

Ingredients
2.2 lbs. (1 kg) chicken thighs
1 ½ tsp. kosher salt
1 tsp. garlic powder
½ tsp. freshly ground black pepper
½ tsp. paprika
8 pieces corn on the cob
½ cup (120 g) butter, softened

Method
1. Mix together 1 teaspoon salt, garlic powder, pepper, and paprika in a small bowl. Place chicken thighs in a non-reactive baking dish and rub with this mixture. Cover and refrigerate for at least 3 hours to absorb the flavor.
2. Heat the grill to medium-high.
3. Cook chicken until cooked through, turning often to cook evenly.
4. Add the corn on the grill and cook for 15 minutes or until cooked through.
5. Transfer chicken and corn to a serving dish; brush with softened butter. Season to taste with remaining salt.
6. Serve and enjoy.

Nutritional Information:
Energy - 324 kcal; Fat – 18.3 g; Carbs – 14.5 g; Protein – 26.8 g; Sodium – 596 mg

Grilled Herbed Salmon

Preparation Time: 12 minutes; **Total Time:** 30 minutes; **Yield:** 8 servings

Ingredients
2 Tbsp. (15 ml) olive oil
2 Tbsp. (15 ml) lemon juice
1/4 cup (15 g) mixed chopped fresh herbs
4 (5 oz. or 150 g) salmon steaks

1/2 tsp. (2.5 g) sea salt
1/4 tsp. (1 g) ground black pepper
cooking oil spray

Method
1. Grease grill grate with oil spray. Preheat grill to medium-high heat.
2. Meanwhile, whisk together olive oil, lemon juice, and chopped mixed herbs.
3. Add the salmon and turn to coat all sides. Let stand for a few minutes then add pepper and salt to season it.
4. Cook salmon over a hot grill until cooked through, about 15 minutes, turning halfway through cooking.
5. Transfer to a serving dish.
6. Serve and enjoy.

Nutritional Information:
Energy - 212 kcal; Fat – 14.1 g; Carbs – 0.3 g; Protein – 22.1 g; Sodium – 286 mg

Les Ilagan

Grilled Marinated Salmon on Spinach Bed

Preparation Time: 12 minutes; **Total Time:** 30 minutes; **Yield:** 8 servings

Ingredients
1/4 cup (60 ml) orange juice
3 Tbsp. (45 ml) olive oil, divided
2 tsp. thyme, divided
2.2 lbs. (1 kg) salmon fillets
1 Tbsp. (20 ml) honey
1 Tbsp. (6 g) sweet paprika

1 tsp. (5 g) orange zest, grated
1 tsp. (2 g) ground cinnamon
½ tsp. (2.5 g) kosher salt
1 (10 oz. or 300 g) bag fresh spinach leaves

Method
1. Whisk orange juice, 2 tablespoons oil and 1 teaspoon of thyme in a small bowl. Place salmon in a shallow glass bowl. Add marinade; turn to coat all sides then keep in the fridge for at least 30 minutes covered.
2. Preheat your oven to 400°F (200°C).
3. Combine honey, paprika, orange zest, cinnamon, remaining 1 teaspoon thyme, and sea salt in a small bowl.
4. Remove salmon from marinade. Place in a greased baking pan.
5. Rub salmon evenly with the honey-paprika mixture.
6. Bake in the preheated oven for 12 to 15 minutes or until fish flakes easily with a fork.
7. Meanwhile, heat remaining oil in large skillet over medium flame. Add the spinach and cook 2 minutes or until just wilted.
8. Serve salmon over spinach.

Nutritional Information:
Energy - 219 kcal; Fat – 12.5 g; Carbs – 5.2 g; Protein – 23.2 g; Sodium – 226 mg

Herbed Beef and Vegetable Stew

Preparation Time: 10 minutes; **Total Time:** 30 minutes; **Yield:** 4 servings

Ingredients

2 Tbsp. (30 ml) olive oil
2.2 lbs. (1 kg) beef stew, cubed about 1-inch
3 cups (750 ml) water
1 medium (110 g) onion, chopped
1/2 tsp. (1 g) pepper
1 tsp. (5 g) sea salt
1-½ tsp. (3 g) garlic powder
1 tsp. (2 g) dried rosemary
1 tsp. (2 g) dried oregano
1 tsp. (2 g) dried basil

1 tsp. (2 g) ground marjoram
2 bay leaves
1 can (6 oz. or 180 g) tomato paste
2 cups (400 g) potatoes, peeled and cubed
2 cups (400 g) carrots, sliced
1 medium (125 g) green pepper, chopped
1 package (9 oz. or 270 g) frozen cut green beans
1 package (10 oz. or 280 g) frozen corn
1 cup (150 g) mushrooms, sliced
3 (125 g) tomatoes, chopped

Method

1. Over medium-high heat, heat oil in a Dutch oven and then brown the meat.
2. Add the water, onion, seasonings, herbs, and tomato paste. Simmer while covered until meat is almost tender for 1-½ hours.
3. Add the potatoes, carrots, green pepper, beans, corn, mushrooms, and tomatoes. Cook, covered for another 30 minutes. Add additional water if necessary.
4. Transfer to a serving dish.
5. Serve and enjoy.

Nutritional Information:
Energy - 308 kcal; Fat – 9.5 g; Carbs – 27.3 g; Protein – 30.3 g; Sodium – 396 mg

Herbed Chicken Burger Patties

Preparation Time: 12 minutes; **Total Time:** 30 minutes; **Yield:** 6 servings

Ingredients
1 lb. (450 g) ground chicken breast
1/2 cup (50 g) dry seasoned breadcrumbs
1/2 cup (80 g) onion, finely chopped
1/4 cup (40 g) celery, finely chopped
1 (60 g) whole egg
1/2 tsp. (1 g) dried rosemary
1/2 tsp. (1 g) dried thyme
1/2 tsp. (2.5 g) kosher salt
1/4 tsp. (0.5 g) freshly ground black pepper
vegetable oil, for frying

Method
1. In a large mixing bowl, combine chicken along with the rest of the ingredients. Mix well.
2. Divide mixture and form into 4 balls and press to make burger patties.
3. Over medium-high heat, heat oil in a large pan. Then, cook the chicken burgers in batches until golden brown and cooked through.
4. Transfer to a serving dish.
5. Serve and enjoy.

Nutritional Information:
Energy - 308 kcal; Fat – 12.1 g; Carbs – 11.6 g; Protein – 36.3 g; Sodium – 482 mg

Cheesy Vegetable and Rice Casserole

Preparation Time: 10 minutes; **Total Time:** 30 minutes; **Yield:** 5 servings

Ingredients
2 Tbsp. (30 ml) vegetable oil
1/2 tsp. (2.5 g) kosher salt
1 cup (200 g) extra-long grain rice
2 cups (300 g) frozen mixed vegetables
3 cups (750 ml) chicken stock
1 cup (125 g) cheddar cheese, grated

Method
1. Preheat your oven to 400°F (200°C).
2. Heat oil in a medium saucepan over moderate flame.
3. Add the rest of the ingredients, except for the cheddar cheese.
4. Boil for 1 minute then simmer over low heat while covered for 15 minutes. Transfer to a large casserole dish. Sprinkle with cheddar cheese.
5. Bake in the preheated oven for 15 minutes, or until rice is cooked through and cheese is melted.
6. Serve and enjoy.

Nutritional Information:
Energy - 276 kcal; Fat – 12.1 g; Carbs – 32.8 g; Protein – 9.2 g; Sodium – 414 mg

Les Ilagan

Chicken and Vegetable Stir-Fry

Preparation Time: 12 minutes; **Total Time:** 30 minutes; **Yield:** 8 servings

Ingredients

1 lb. (450 g) skinless, boneless chicken breast, cut into small pieces
2 Tbsp. (30 ml) soy sauce
2 Tbsp. (30 ml) dry sherry
1 Tbsp. (8 g) cornstarch
1 Tbsp. (15 g) canola oil
1 medium (110 g) white onion, chopped
2 cloves (6 g) garlic, minced

1 cup (175 g) broccoli florets, cut into small pieces
1 medium (125 g) red bell pepper, diced
1 medium (60 g) carrot, diced
1 cup (100 g) Brussels sprouts
1/2 cup (120 ml) chicken broth
1 Tbsp. (15 ml) canola oil

Method

1. Combine chicken, soy sauce, sherry, and cornstarch in a medium bowl.
2. Heat 1 tablespoon canola oil in a large pan or skillet over moderate flame. Stir-fry onion and garlic for 3 minutes or until fragrant.
3. Add the broccoli, bell pepper, carrot, Brussels sprouts, and chicken stock; cover, and cook until vegetables are tender. Transfer vegetables to a large bowl and wipe pan clean.
4. Heat remaining 1 tablespoon canola oil over moderate flame. Stir-fry the chicken until meat is cooked through. Stir in vegetables; cook further 2 to 3 minutes more then add pepper and salt.
5. Transfer to a serving dish.
6. Serve and enjoy.

Nutritional Information:

Energy - 248 kcal; Fat – 8.7 g; Carbs – 10.4 g; Protein – 28.9 g; Sodium – 515 mg

SOUTHERN COOKING

Crispy Fried Chicken Wings

Preparation Time: 10 minutes; **Total Time:** 30 minutes; **Yield:** 4 servings

Ingredients
1 (60 g) large egg
1 cup (250 ml) buttermilk
2 lbs. (1 kg) chicken wings, split and tips removed
1 ½ cups (180 g) all-purpose flour
1/2 cup (60 g) crushed saltine crackers
1/2 tsp. (1 g) ground black pepper
1/2 tsp. (1 g) dried rosemary
1/2 tsp. (1 g) sweet paprika
1/2 tsp. (2.5 g) salt
1/2 tsp. (1 g) garlic powder
cooking oil, for frying
salt and ground black pepper to taste

Method
1. Whisk together the eggs and 1 cup buttermilk in a mixing bowl. Add the chicken wings, cover, and refrigerate 30 minutes. Combine the flour and crushed crackers with the pepper, rosemary, paprika, salt, and garlic powder in a separate large mixing bowl.
2. Heat oil in a deep-frying pan.
3. Separate chicken wings from the buttermilk marinade then coat well with the breadcrumb mixture.
4. Fry breaded chicken wings in hot oil in batches until golden brown on the outside and cooked through, about 10 minutes. Drain on a paper towel-lined plate.
5. Serve and enjoy.

Nutritional Information:
Energy - 335 kcal; Fat – 15.3 g; Carbs – 15.3 g; Protein – 31.6 g; Sodium – 302 mg

Pasta and Chicken Sausage in Tomato Sauce

Preparation Time: 20 minutes; **Total Time:** 1 hour; **Yield:** 6 servings

Ingredients

1 (8 oz.) package pasta (you can use any pasta that you like)
1 Tbsp. (15 ml) canola oil
1 lb. (450 g) chicken sausage, thinly sliced
1 medium (110 g) onion, thinly sliced
1 (14.5 oz.) can diced tomatoes
1 Tbsp. (3.5 g) fresh basil, chopped
1 Tbsp. (3.5 g) fresh oregano, chopped
1 cup (120 g) cheddar cheese, shredded

Method

1. Preheat oven to 400°F (200°C).
2. Bring a large stockpot of lightly salted water to a boil. Cook pasta as directed in the package directions. Drain.
3. Heat oil in a large saucepan over medium-high flame. Stir-fry onion for 3 minutes. Add the chicken sausage and cook, stirring for 5-7 minutes.
4. Stir in diced tomatoes, basil, and oregano. Cook further 5 minutes.
5. Add the pasta. Mix well. Transfer to a baking dish. Sprinkle with cheese.
6. Bake in the oven for about 15 minutes, or until cheese has melted.
7. Serve and enjoy.

Nutritional Information:

Energy - 371 kcal; Fat – 20.4 g; Carbs – 26.7 g; Protein – 28.2 g; Sodium - 443 mg

SIDES

Zucchini and Cabbage Casserole

Preparation Time: 20 minutes; **Total Time:** 55 minutes; **Yield:** 8 servings

Ingredients
2.2 lbs. (1 kg) zucchini, thinly sliced
10.75 oz. can (306 g) condensed cream of chicken soup
1 small (400 g) head cabbage, shredded
1 medium (110 g) onion, thinly sliced
1 cup (250 g) plain yogurt
1 cup (100 g) seasoned breadcrumbs
1/2 cup (125 g) unsalted butter, melted
1/2 cup (60 g) cheddar cheese, grated

Method
1. Preheat oven to 400°F (200°C).
2. Boil the sliced zucchini, cabbage, and onion in water for about 5 minutes. Drain well.
3. Combine the chicken soup and yogurt in a medium bowl.
4. Add in the zucchini mixture into the soup mixture. Mix well.
5. In a separate medium bowl, mix together the butter and seasoned breadcrumbs. Take half of this mixture and spread into the bottom of a 9x13-inch baking dish. Pour the zucchini mixture, then top with the other half of the breadcrumb mixture. Sprinkle with cheddar cheese.
6. Bake in the oven for 20-25 minutes, or until it is golden brown. Cool slightly.
7. Serve and enjoy.

Nutritional Information:
Energy - 273 kcal; Fat – 16.2 g; Carbs – 25.5 g; Protein – 9.3 g; Sodium - 424 mg

Les Ilagan

Cheesy Eggplant and Tomato Casserole with Herbs

Preparation Time: 20 minutes; **Total Time:** 50 minutes; **Yield:** 8 servings

Ingredients

2.2 lbs. (1 kg) eggplant (thinly sliced)
2 cups (300 g) cherry tomatoes (halved)
10.75 oz. can (306 g) condensed cream of mushroom soup
1 cup (250 g) plain yogurt
1 Tbsp. (3.5 g) fresh rosemary, chopped
1 Tbsp. (3.5 g) fresh basil, chopped

1 Tbsp. (15 g) parmesan cheese
1 tsp. (2 g) garlic powder
1 cup (250 g) ready-made chicken stuffing mix
1/2 cup (125 g) unsalted butter, melted
1/2 cup (60 g) cheddar cheese, grated

Method

1. Preheat the oven to 380°F (190°C). Season the eggplant slices with salt and let sit for about 10 minutes. Drain off the liquid.
2. In a medium bowl, mix together mushroom soup, yogurt, rosemary, basil, parmesan, and garlic powder. Mix well. Stir in eggplant and cherry tomatoes.
3. In a separate bowl, combine stuffing mix and butter. Take half of this mixture and spread into the bottom of a 9x13-inch casserole dish or baking dish. Pour the eggplant mixture, then top with the other half of the stuffing mixture. Sprinkle with cheddar cheese.
4. Bake in the oven for 25-30 minutes, or until eggplant is cooked through. Cool slightly.
5. Serve and enjoy.

Nutritional Information:

Energy - 279 kcal; Fat – 17.4 g; Carbs – 24.3 g; Protein – 8.0 g; Sodium - 478 mg

Homemade Vegetarian Casserole

Preparation Time: 15 minutes; **Total Time:** 50 minutes; **Yield:** 6 servings

Ingredients

1 medium (400 g) broccoli head, separated into florets
1 medium (400 g) cauliflower separated into florets
1 medium (60 g) carrot, diced
10.75 oz. can (306 g) condensed cream of mushroom soup
1 cup (120 g) shredded cheddar cheese (divided)
1/2 cup (125 g) sour cream
1/2 cup (50 g) breadcrumbs
freshly ground black pepper

Method

1. Preheat oven to 380°F (190°C).
2. Blanch vegetables in boiling water for 5 minutes. Drain and set aside.
3. In a large bowl combine mushroom soup, half of the cheddar cheese, sour cream, and breadcrumbs then add pepper and salt to season it.
4. Add the broccoli, cauliflower, and carrot. Mix well before transferring to a 9x13-inch casserole dish.
5. Turn into the preheated oven for 25 minutes then add the remaining cheese on top. Bake for another 10 minutes before removing from heat and cooling slightly.
6. Serve and enjoy.

Nutritional Information:

Energy - 229 kcal; Fat – 14.2 g; Carbs – 18.6 g; Protein – 10.9 g; Sodium - 529 mg

Cheesy Mushroom and Potato Bake

Preparation Time: 15 minutes; **Total Time:** 40 minutes; **Yield:** 4 servings

Ingredients
4 medium (800 g) boiled potatoes, cubed
2 Tbsp. (30 g) unsalted butter
1 medium (110 g) onion, chopped
1 ½ cup (225 g) button mushrooms, halved
1/2 cup (125 g) cream of mushroom soup
2 Tbsp. (30 g) sour cream
1/4 cup (30 g) cheddar cheese, grated

Method
1. Preheat oven to 400°F (200°C).
2. Over medium-low flame, melt butter in a large pan; then stir-fry onion for 5 minutes or until tender.
3. Add the mushrooms, cream of mushroom, and sour cream. Cook further 3-5 minutes, stirring frequently.
4. Place potatoes in a baking dish. Pour the mushroom mixture over potatoes and sprinkle with cheddar cheese.
5. Bake for 10-12 minutes. Cool slightly.
6. Serve and enjoy.

Nutritional Information:
Energy - 297 kcal; Fat – 13.4 g; Carbs – 38.2 g; Protein – 9.7 g; Sodium - 244 mg

Green Bean Casserole with Cheddar

Preparation Time: 10 minutes; **Total Time:** 45 minutes; **Yield:** 6 servings

Ingredients
1 ½ lb. (675 g) fresh green beans (trimmed, cut into 2-inch pieces, and blanched)
10.75 oz. can (306 g) condensed cream of chicken soup
1/2 cup (125 g) sour cream
1 tsp. (2 g) onion powder
1/2 cup (60 g) cheddar cheese, grated
freshly ground black pepper

Method
1. Preheat oven to 350°F.
2. Combine the chicken soup, sour cream, and onion powder in a large bowl. Add the blanched green beans. Mix well. Season with pepper to taste.
3. Transfer to a baking dish. Bake for 20 minutes. Sprinkle with cheddar cheese and cook further 10 minutes. Cool slightly.
4. Serve and enjoy.

Nutritional Information:
Energy - 157 kcal; Fat – 8.3 g; Carbs – 16.4 g; Protein – 7.3 g; Sodium - 281 mg

Les Ilagan

Creamy Baked Macaroni and Cheese

Preparation Time: 10 minutes; **Total Time:** 52 minutes; **Yield:** 6 servings

Ingredients

2 Tbsp. (30 g) unsalted butter
1 medium (110 g) onion, finely chopped
2 Tbsp. (15 g) all-purpose flour
2 cups (500 ml) milk
1/2 tsp. (1 g) garlic powder
1/2 tsp. (1 g) dry mustard
1/4 tsp. (0.5 g) freshly ground black pepper
12 oz. (360 g) package elbow macaroni
1 cup (120 g) sharp cheddar cheese, grated
1 cup (120 g) American cheese, grated

Method

1. Preheat oven to 380°F (190°C).
2. In a pot, boil a of lightly salted water then add macaroni noodles and cook as directed in the package directions. Drain. Set aside.
3. Over medium-low flame, heat butter in a large pan; then stir-fry onion for 3 minutes.
4. Add the flour and cook for 1 minute, stirring constantly.
5. Next, add in milk, garlic powder, mustard, and pepper and constantly stir until thick.
6. Add the cheeses and stir until melted.
7. Add the cooked macaroni and mix well. Transfer to a 2-quart baking dish.
8. For 20 minutes, bake in the preheated oven. Cool slightly before serving.
9. Enjoy.

Nutritional Information:

Energy - 395 kcal; Fat – 16.5 g; Carbs – 39.9 g; Protein – 18.6 g; Sodium - 436 mg

SOUTHERN COOKING

Broccoli Pasta and Cheese Bake

Preparation Time: 15 minutes; **Total Time:** 45 minutes; **Yield:** 8 servings

Ingredients

8 oz. (250 g) pasta, macaroni or fusilli
1/3 cup (85 g) unsalted butter
1/3 cup (40 g) all-purpose flour
3 cups (750 g) whole milk
1/4 cup (30 g) parmesan cheese, grated
1 tsp. (2 g) garlic powder
1/4 tsp. nutmeg, ground

1/2 tsp. (1 g) sage, dried
1 cup (120 g) sharp cheddar cheese, grated
1 ½ lb. (675 g) fresh broccoli (steamed)
1/4 cup (30 g) Swiss cheese (grated)
freshly ground black pepper
cooking oil spray

Method

1. Preheat oven to 380°F (190°C). Lightly grease a 9x13 inch baking dish with oil spray.
2. Cook the pasta until al dente in a large pot of boiling salted water. Drain.
3. In the meantime, melt butter in a large saucepan over medium flame. Add the flour and milk and cook until the mixture becomes thick, stirring often.
4. Stir in grated parmesan, garlic powder, nutmeg, sage, and cheddar.
5. Add steamed broccoli and pasta to the cheese sauce. Mix well. Pour into the prepared baking dish. Sprinkle with grated Swiss cheese.
6. Bake in the oven, uncovered, for 20-30 minutes. Cool slightly.
7. Serve and enjoy.

Nutritional Information:

Energy - 331 kcal; Fat – 16.8 g; Carbs – 30.1 g; Protein – 16.5 g; Sodium - 277 mg

Macaroni Mushroom and Cheese Casserole

Preparation Time: 12 minutes; **Total Time:** 30 minutes; **Yield:** 8 servings

Ingredients
1 cup (125 g) shredded cheddar cheese
1 can (10-3/4 oz. or 300 g) condensed cream of mushroom soup
1 cup (250 g) light mayonnaise
1 can (7 oz. or 200 g) mushroom stems and pieces, drained
1 medium (110 g) onion, finely chopped
1 jar (2 oz. or 60 g) diced pimientos, drained
1 lb. (450 g) elbow macaroni, cooked
1 clove (3 g) garlic, minced
salt and freshly ground black pepper

Method
1. In a large bowl, mix well pimientos, onion, mushrooms, mayonnaise, cream of mushroom soup, and cheddar cheese.
2. Stir in macaroni and garlic. Transfer mixture to a greased baking dish. Cover and bake at 350°F (175°C) for 20 to 30 minutes or until heated through and cheese is melted. Cool slightly.
3. Serve and enjoy.

Nutritional Information:
Energy - 349 kcal; Fat – 22.8 g; Carbs – 27.3 g; Protein – 10.1 g; Sodium – 1017 mg

SOUTHERN COOKING

Sweet Potato Casserole with Pecan

Preparation Time: 15 minutes; **Total Time:** 45 minutes; **Yield:** 8 servings

Ingredients
5 cups (1250 g) sweet potatoes (cooked and mashed)
1/4 cup (30 g) butter, melted
1/3 cup (85 ml) milk
1/3 cup (75 g) white sugar
2 (60 g) whole eggs, beaten
1 tsp. (2 g) cinnamon (ground)
1/4 tsp. (1.5 g) Kosher salt

cooking oil spray

Pecan Streusel Topping:
2/3 cup (145 g) light brown sugar
1/2 cup (60 g) all-purpose flour
1/4 cup (30 g) butter
1/2 tsp. (1 g) nutmeg (ground)
1 cup (100 g) pecans (coarsely chopped)

Method
1. Preheat oven to 350°F (175°C).
2. In a large bowl, combine mashed sweet potatoes, melted butter, milk, white sugar, eggs, and cinnamon then spread the mixture into a greased 9x13-inch baking dish.
3. In another bowl, prepare the streusel topping by mixing together the brown sugar, flour, butter, and nutmeg. Mix well. Stir in the pecans.
4. Top the sweet potato mixture with the pecan mixture then bake for 25 minutes in the preheated oven.
5. Cool slightly then serve and enjoy.

Nutritional Information:
Energy - 384 kcal; Fat – 18.2 g; Carbs – 54.3 g; Protein – 5.6 g; Sodium - 188 mg

Les Ilagan

Easy Succotash Recipe

Preparation Time: 10 minutes; **Total Time:** 26 minutes; **Yield:** 4 servings

Ingredients
3 Tbsp. (45 g) butter
2 cups (300 g) green beans (trimmed then divided into 2-inch portions)
1 cup (170 g) frozen peas (thawed)
1 cup (165 g) sweetcorn kernels
1 medium (60 g) carrot, peeled and diced
1/2 tsp. (2.5 g) sugar
Kosher salt and freshly ground pepper

Method
1. Melt 3 tablespoons butter in a skillet over medium flame. Then, add the green beans, frozen peas, corn, and carrot. Cook until crisp-tender, about 10 minutes, stirring often.
2. Add the sugar, pepper, and salt. Remove from heat.
3. Transfer to a serving dish.
4. Serve immediately and enjoy.

Nutritional Information:
Energy - 166 kcal; Fat – 9.3 g; Carbs – 19.0 g; Protein – 5.5 g; Sodium - 257 mg

SOUTHERN COOKING

Steamed Vegetable Medley

Preparation Time: 10 minutes; **Total Time:** 40 minutes; **Yield:** 4 servings

Ingredients
10 oz. (300 g) Brussels sprouts
2 cups (240 g) broccoli florets
1 large (100 g) carrot, cut into strips
1 medium (125 g) red bell pepper, deseeded and thinly sliced

1 cup (170 g) frozen green peas (thawed)
2 tablespoons (30 ml) lemon juice
salt and freshly ground black pepper

Method
1. In a steamer, boil water.
2. Place the Brussels sprouts, broccoli florets, carrots, red bell pepper, and peas in a steamer basket. Put into the steamer then cook covered for 10 minutes until tender. Remove from heat.
3. Transfer steamed vegetables to a large bowl, Drizzle with lemon juice and season with salt and pepper to taste. Toss to coat.
4. Serve immediately and enjoy.

Nutritional Information:
Energy - 93 kcal; Fat – 0.3 g; Carbs – 19.2 g; Protein – 5.9 g; Sodium - 195 mg

SALADS

Creamy Potato Egg and Onion Salad

Preparation Time: 30 minutes; **Total Time:** 2 hours 50 minutes; **Yield:** 8 servings

Ingredients

6 boiled eggs, peeled and chopped
10 medium (2 kg) red potatoes
1 cup (250 g) light mayonnaise
125 (g) cup ranch dressing
1/3 cup dill pickle relish
2 Tbsp. (30 g) Dijon mustard
1/2 tsp. (1 g) paprika
1/2 tsp. (1 g) coriander seed, ground
1 medium (100 g) red onion, chopped
salt and freshly ground black pepper

Method

1. Over high flame, boil potatoes in a large pot or saucepan. Lower the heat to medium. Cover with lid and cook until tender, about 15 to 20 minutes. Completely drain before keeping it in the fridge to cool. Peel the potatoes and cube once cold.
2. Mix together the light mayonnaise, ranch dressing, pickle relish, Dijon mustard, paprika, and coriander in a large mixing bowl.
3. Add the eggs, potatoes, and onion. Toss to combine well then add pepper and salt to season it. Keep it in the fridge until ready to serve for about 2 hours.
4. Transfer to a serving dish.
5. Serve immediately and enjoy.

Nutritional Information:

Energy - 374 kcal; Fat – 14.1 g; Carbs – 55.7 g; Protein – 10.4 g; Sodium - 557 mg

Garden Fresh Salad with Roasted Chicken Breast

Preparation Time: 10 minutes; **Total Time:** 10 minutes; **Yield:** 4 servings

Ingredients
4 cups (240 g) baby spinach
1 (200 g) head lettuce, torn
2 cups (300 g) cherry tomatoes (halved)
1 medium (200 g) cucumber (thinly sliced)
1 medium (110 g) red onion (thinly sliced)
12 oz. (360 g) roasted chicken breast fillet, thinly sliced
salt and freshly ground black pepper

Lemon Vinaigrette with Honey:
1/3 cup (85 ml) olive oil
1/4 cup (60 ml) lemon juice
1 Tbsp. (20 ml) honey

Method
1. Prepare the dressing by mixing together the olive oil, lemon juice, and honey in a small bowl.
2. Place the spinach, lettuce, cherry tomatoes, cucumber, and onion in a large bowl. Toss to combine.
3. Divide salad among serving plates. Top with roasted chicken and drizzle with dressing.
4. You may serve immediately or keep it refrigerated until ready to consume.
5. Enjoy.

Nutritional Information:
Energy - 230 kcal; Fat – 12.8 g; Carbs – 11.2 g; Protein – 18.5 g; Sodium - 171 mg

Red Cabbage and Carrot Slaw with Mango

Preparation Time: 15 minutes; **Total Time:** 6 hours 30 minutes; **Yield:** 5 servings

Ingredients

1/4 cup (60 ml) olive oil
1/3 cup (85 ml) red wine vinegar
1 Tbsp. (20 ml) honey
1/2 tsp. (1 g) onion powder
1/2 tsp. (2.5 g) Kosher salt

1/4 tsp. (0.5 g) freshly ground black pepper
1 Tbsp. (3.5 g) dill weed, chopped
1 head (300 g) red cabbage, cored and shredded
2 cups (330 g) ripe mango, diced

Method

1. In a large bowl, mix together the olive oil, red wine vinegar, honey, onion powder, salt, pepper, and dill.
2. Add the cabbage and mango. Toss to coat. Cover with plastic wrap and refrigerate for at least 4 hours, stirring occasionally.
3. Serve immediately and enjoy.

Nutritional Information:

Energy - 221 kcal; Fat – 11.3 g; Carbs – 33.2 g; Protein – 3.4 g; Sodium – 146 mg

Coleslaw with Apple and Scallions

Preparation Time: 15 minutes; **Total Time:** 2 hours 15 minutes; **Yield:** 5 servings

Ingredients

1/3 cup (85 g) sour cream
1/3 cup (85 g) mayonnaise
2 Tbsp. (30 g) Dijon mustard
1 Tbsp. (20 ml) honey
1 Tbsp. (15 ml) white wine vinegar
2 (180 g) green apples, cored and diced
2 (180 g) red apples, cored and diced
3 cups (210 g) cabbage, shredded
1 large (100 g) carrot, shredded
1 medium (110 g) red onion, chopped
1/4 cup (15 g) fresh flat-leaf parsley, chopped

Method

1. In a large bowl, combine the sour cream, mayonnaise, Dijon mustard, honey, and white wine vinegar.
2. Add the apples, cabbage, carrot, onion, and fresh parsley. Season to taste. Toss to mix thoroughly. Cover and keep refrigerated for 2 hours or until ready to serve.
3. Enjoy.

Nutritional Information:

Energy - 231 kcal; Fat – 9.1 g; Carbs – 39.0 g; Protein – 2.4 g; Sodium – 329 mg

Fresh Green Salad with Smoked Salmon

Preparation Time: 10 minutes; **Total Time:** 30 minutes; **Yield:** 4 servings

Ingredients

1/4 cup (60 ml) extra-virgin olive oil
2 Tbsp. (30 ml) fresh lemon juice
2 Tbsp. (7 g) fresh dill, chopped
10 oz. (300 g) leafy greens (baby rocket and, lettuce)
6 oz. (180 g) thinly sliced smoked salmon, cut into 1/2-inch ribbons
1 lmedium (110 g) red onion, thinly sliced
6 oz. (180 g) cherry tomatoes, halved
2 Tbsp. (20 g) capers
kosher salt and freshly ground pepper

Method
1. Whisk olive oil along with lemon juice and dill in a small bowl then add pepper and salt to season it.
2. Place leafy greens, cherry tomatoes, onion slices, salmon, and capers in a large salad bowl then keep it chilled and covered until ready to consume.
3. Serve salad drizzled with dressing.

Nutritional Information:
Energy - 209 kcal; Fat – 15.1 g; Carbs – 10.4 g; Protein – 11.2 g; Sodium – 936 mg

Spinach Salad with Shrimp and Persimmon

Preparation Time: 25 minutes; **Total Time:** 1 hour 15 minutes; **Yield:** 4 servings

Ingredients

1 (10 oz. or 300 g) package baby spinach leaves
1 lb. (450 g) cooked shrimps
2 persimmons (cut thinly into small pieces)

1/4 cup (60 ml) extra-virgin olive oil
2 Tbsp. (30 ml) red wine vinegar
freshly ground black pepper to taste

Method

1. In a large bowl, add the spinach, shrimp, and persimmons. Mix thoroughly.
2. In a small bowl, whisk together olive oil and red wine vinegar.
3. Drizzle vinegar mixture over salad then add pepper and salt.
4. Toss well then keep it chilled until ready to serve.
5. Enjoy.

Nutritional Information:

Energy - 277 kcal; Fat – 14.4 g; Carbs – 9.3 g; Protein – 28.2 g; Sodium – 380 mg

Les Ilagan

Fresh Peach Salsa

Preparation Time: 15 minutes; **Total Time:** 15 minutes; **Yield:** 6 servings

Ingredients
1/4 cup (60 ml) olive oil
3 Tbsp. (45 ml) lime juice
1 Tbsp. (20 ml) honey
1 clove (3 g) garlic, minced
2 cups (300 g) cherry tomatoes, chopped
2 cups (300 g) peaches, chopped
1 medium (125 g) green bell pepper, chopped
1 medium (110 g) white onion, chopped
1 Tbsp. (3.5 g) fresh coriander, finely chopped
1/2 tsp. (2.5 g) Kosher salt
1/4 tsp. (0.5 g) freshly ground black pepper

Method
1. Whisk together olive oil, lime juice, honey, and garlic in a large bowl.
2. Add the cherry tomatoes, peaches, green bell pepper, onion, and fresh coriander then add pepper and salt.
3. Toss well keep it chilled while covered in plastic wrap until ready to consume.
4. Enjoy.

Nutritional Information:
Energy - 130 kcal; Fat – 9.0 g; Carbs – 14.4 g; Protein – 2.5 g; Sodium – 105 mg

SNACKS

Homemade Spinach Cornbread

Preparation Time: 12 minutes; **Total Time:** 45 minutes; **Yield:** 10 servings

Ingredients

1 (10 oz. or 300 g) package of frozen spinach (thawed, chopped, and squeezed dry)
1 (8 oz. or 250 g) can of cream-style corn
1 cup (250 g) low-fat sour cream
2 (60 g) large eggs, beaten
1/4 cup (60 g) butter, melted
1 package (240 g) package corn muffin mix
cooking oil spray

Method

1. Preheat oven to 350°F (175°C). Lightly grease a 9-inch square baking dish with oil spray.
2. In a large bowl, mix together the spinach, corn, sour cream, eggs, and butter until well combined. Stir in 1 package dry cornbread mix. Pour this mixture into the prepared pan and spread evenly using a spatula.
3. Bake in the oven for 35 minutes, or until firm and golden brown on the top. Cool a wire rack before cutting into portions.
4. Serve and enjoy.

Nutritional Information:
Energy - 217 kcal; Fat – 12.6 g; Carbs – 23.2 g; Protein – 5.3 g; Sodium – 351 mg

Southern-Style Yellow Cornbread

Preparation Time: 15 minutes; **Total Time:** 45 minutes; **Yield:** 10 servings

Ingredients
1 stick (125 g) butter
2 (60 g) large eggs
1 cup (250 ml) buttermilk
1/2 tsp. (3 g) baking soda

1 cup (175 g) cornmeal
1 cup (125 g) all-purpose flour
1/2 tsp. (2.5 g) salt

Method
1. Preheat oven to 380°F (190°C).
2. Melt butter in a large saucepan. Remove from heat. Stir in the sugar and eggs, quickly beat until well blended.
3. In a small bowl, mix together buttermilk and baking soda. Then, add into the saucepan.
4. Add the cornmeal, all-purpose flour, and salt until well blended and only a few lumps are left. Transfer to a lightly greased 8-inch square pan.
5. Bake in the preheated oven, until tested done for 30 minutes.
6. Remove from heat and cool slightly before slicing.
7. Serve and enjoy.

Nutritional Information:
Energy - 195 kcal; Fat – 11.4 g; Carbs – 20.2 g; Protein – 5.1 g; Sodium – 289 mg

Quick & Easy Choco Almond Scones

Preparation Time: 15 minutes; **Total Time:** 35 minutes; **Yield:** 12 servings

Ingredients

2 cups (250 g) all-purpose flour
1/3 cup (75 g) brown sugar, packed
1 ½ tsp. (6 g) baking powder
1/2 tsp. (3 g) baking soda
1/4 tsp. (1.5 g) salt
1/3 cup (85 g) butter, unsalted

1/2 cup (125 ml) buttermilk
1 (60 ml) large egg
1 ½ tsp. (7.5 ml) almond extract
1 cup (165 g) semisweet chocolate chips
1/2 cup (50 g) dry roasted almonds, chopped

Method

1. Preheat oven to 400°F (200°C). Grease a 9-inch circle in the middle of a baking sheet with butter.
2. In a large mixing bowl, mix the flour, brown sugar, baking powder, baking soda, and salt together.
3. Cut the butter into small cubes, and place evenly over flour mixture. With a pastry cutter, combine the flour mixture and butter.
4. Add the buttermilk, egg, and almond extract. Mix well. Fold in the chocolate chips and almonds. The resulting dough will be sticky.
5. Place the dough into the 9-inch diameter circle on the baking sheet. Cut with a serrated knife to make 12 equal wedges.
6. Bake in the oven for 18 to 20 minutes, or until the top is golden brown. Cool slightly. Cut into wedges.
7. Serve warm and enjoy.

Nutritional Information:

Energy - 265 kcal; Fat – 13.3 g; Carbs – 34.1 g; Protein – 4.0 g; Sodium – 157 mg

Les Ilagan

Pumpkin Scones with Raisins and Walnuts

Preparation Time: 25 minutes; **Total Time:** 1 hour 40 minutes; **Yield:** 12 servings

Ingredients
1 ¾ cups (220 g) all-purpose flour
1/4 cup (55 g) brown sugar
1 Tbsp. (2 g) baking powder
1/2 tsp. (3 g) baking soda
1/4 tsp. (1.5 g) salt
1/3 cup (75 g) cold unsalted butter, cut into pieces
1/2 cup (125 g) pumpkin puree
1/3 cup buttermilk
1/2 cup (60 g) seedless raisins
1/2 cup (50g) walnuts (coarsely chopped)
2 Tbsp. (15 g) whole wheat flour + extra if necessary
1 (60 g) large egg
1 tsp. (5 ml) whole milk
1 tsp. (5 g) white sugar

Method
1. Preheat the oven to 400°F (200°C).
2. Combine 1 3/4 cup flour, 1/4 cup brown sugar, baking powder, baking soda, and salt in a large mixing bowl. Mix well. Using a pastry cutter, add the butter into the flour mixture, until the mixture forms coarse crumbs.
3. Make a well in the middle then stir in pumpkin puree, buttermilk, raisins, and walnuts until just combined.
4. Sprinkle a work surface with 2 tablespoons whole wheat flour. Transfer dough onto the floured work surface. Shape into a 9-inch diameter round dough and place onto lined baking sheet. Using a knife cut into 12 equal wedges.
5. Combine egg and whole milk together in a small bowl. Lightly brush the top of scone with this egg wash mixture and then sprinkle with sugar.
6. Bake in the oven until lightly browned, about 17 to 18 minutes. Remove from heat and place into a wire rack to cool then serve and enjoy.

Nutritional Information:
Energy - 193 kcal; Fat – 9.0 g; Carbs – 25.2 g; Protein – 4.3 g; Sodium – 131 mg

SOUTHERN COOKING

Homemade Buttermilk Biscuits

Preparation Time: 20 minutes; **Total Time:** 35 minutes; **Yield:** 12 servings

Ingredients
2 cups (250 g) all-purpose flour
2 tsp. (8 g) baking powder
1/2 tsp. (2.5 g) Kosher salt
1/2 tsp. (3 g) baking soda or bicarbonate of soda

1/3 cup (85 g) unsalted butter (chilled and cut into small slices)
3/4 cup (185 ml) cold buttermilk + 2 Tbsp. (for brushing)

Method
1. Preheat oven to 420°F (210°C).
2. Mix flour, baking powder, salt, and baking soda together in a large bowl.
3. With a pastry cutter, combine the butter into the flour mixture until it becomes coarse crumbs, about 5 minutes.
4. Make a well in the middle of this butter-flour mixture.
5. Pour ¾ cup buttermilk. Mix until just combined.
6. Transfer dough onto floured work surface; pat together to form a rectangle.
7. Fold the rectangle in thirds then turn halfway and flatten back into a rectangle to collect any crumbs during the process. Repeat procedure twice more, folding and pressing dough each time, a total of three times.
8. Roll out the dough on a floured surface to about ½-inch thick.
9. Using a 2 ½-inch round biscuit cutter, cut out 12 biscuits.
10. Place biscuits on lined baking sheet then gently press your thumb, on top of each biscuit to test if it's ready to bake. It should leave a small indent.
11. Brush the biscuit tops with 2 tablespoons buttermilk.
12. Bake in the oven until browned, about 15 minutes.
13. Cool slightly. Serve and enjoy.

Nutritional Information:
Energy - 129 kcal; Fat – 6.0 g; Carbs – 17.4 g; Protein – 3.6 g; Sodium – 181 mg

Les Ilagan

Breadsticks with Parmesan and Herbs

Preparation Time: 10 minutes; **Total Time:** 30 minutes; **Yield:** 12 servings

Ingredients

1/4 cup (30 g) grated parmesan cheese
2 tsp. (4 g) dried basil
1 tsp. (2 g) garlic powder

1 lb. (450 g) frozen bread dough, thawed
2 Tbsp. (30 g) butter, melted
1 tsp. (5 g) kosher salt

Method

1. Combine the parmesan, basil, and garlic powder in a small bowl.
2. Cut bread dough into 24 pieces. Roll each piece into a 12-inch rope. Sprinkle evenly with parmesan mixture.
3. Arrange the ropes, 1-inch apart, on lightly greased baking sheets. Allow to rise at room temperature for 20 minutes while cover in plastic wrap.
4. Bake at 350°F (175°C) until golden brown for 15 minutes then brush with the melted butter. Top with kosher salt then allow to cool on a wire rack.
5. Serve and enjoy.

Nutritional Information:
Energy - 127 kcal; Fat – 4.1 g; Carbs – 19.2 g; Protein – 4.2 g; Sodium – 418 mg

Polenta Sticks with Cheddar

Preparation Time: 15 minutes; **Total Time:** 1 hour 30 minutes; **Yield:** 6 servings

Ingredients

3 ¼ cups (815 ml) cold water
1 cup (170 g) regular polenta (not quick cooking)
1 tsp. (2 g) fresh thyme (chopped)
1 tsp. (2 g) fresh rosemary (chopped)
1/2 tsp. (1 g) paprika
1/2 tsp. (1 g) coriander seed, ground
1/2 cup (60 g) grated cheddar cheese
1 oz. (30 g) unsalted butter, cut into bits
cooking oil spray

Method

1. Grease an 8-inch square baking dish with oil spray.
2. In a large saucepan over medium heat, boil together the following ingredients while whisking - water, polenta, thyme, rosemary, paprika, and coriander. Reduce heat to medium-low and cook, stirring constantly with a long wooden spoon, until the polenta begins to pull away from the sides, about 15 to 20 minutes. Stir in half of the cheese and butter until blended well. Season with salt and pepper to taste. Transfer polenta mixture onto the prepared baking dish. Spread evenly with a dampened spatula. Chill, uncovered, for 45 minutes or until fully set.
3. Preheat your broiler. Spray a baking sheet with oil.
4. Remove polenta from the baking dish, then cut into 16 sticks (about 4x1-inch).
5. Arrange the polenta sticks in the baking sheet in a single layer. Spray with oil.
6. Broil for 15 to 20 minutes, or until golden brown. Cool slightly.
7. Transfer to a serving platter and sprinkle with remaining cheese.
8. Serve enjoy.

Nutritional Information:

Energy - 170 kcal; Fat – 8.2 g; Carbs – 20.1 g; Protein – 4.5 g; Sodium – 187 mg

Homemade Buttered Corn Muffins

Preparation Time: 10 minutes; **Total Time:** 30 minutes; **Yield:** 10 servings

Ingredients
1 cup (170 g) cornmeal
1 cup (125 g) all-purpose flour
1/3 cup (75 g) white sugar
2 tsp. (8 g) baking powder

1/4 tsp. (1.5 g) salt
1 (60 g) large egg, beaten
1/4 cup (60 g) butter, softened
1 cup (250 ml) buttermilk

Method
1. Preheat oven to 400°F (200°C). Grease muffin pan by brushing it with butter.
2. Combine cornmeal, all-purpose flour, sugar, baking powder and salt in a large mixing bowl.
3. Stir in beaten egg, softened butter, and buttermilk. Mix until just combined. Transfer batter into prepared muffin pan.
4. Bake until a toothpick inserted at the center of a muffin comes out clean, about 20 minutes.
5. Cool slightly then serve and enjoy.

Nutritional Information:
Energy - 166 kcal; Fat – 7.2 g; Carbs – 21.3 g; Protein – 4.8 g; Sodium – 91 mg

SOUTHERN COOKING

Egg Salad on Toasts

Preparation Time: 10 minutes; **Total Time:** 30 minutes; **Yield:** 12 servings

Ingredients
5 hard-boiled eggs, chopped
1 shallot, minced
3/4 cup (180 g) light mayonnaise
1 Tbsp. (15 g) Dijon mustard
1 Tbsp. (15 ml) lemon juice
2 Tbsp. (7 g) parsley, chopped
1 baguette (250 g), cut into 12 slices crosswise
salt and freshly ground black pepper

Method
1. In a medium bowl, combine chopped eggs, shallot, mayonnaise, Dijon mustard, lemon juice, and parsley then add pepper and salt.
2. Place bread slices into the toaster oven; toast until golden brown.
3. Equally divide the egg salad mixture and spread evenly into each toasted layer.
4. Serve and enjoy.

Nutritional Information:
Energy - 162 kcal; Fat – 7.4 g; Carbs – 18.3 g; Protein – 6.0 g; Sodium – 423 mg

Les Ilagan

Homemade Chicken Nuggets

Preparation Time: 12 minutes; **Total Time:** 30 minutes; **Yield:** 8 servings

Ingredients
1 cup (125 g) all-purpose flour
1 Tbsp. (6 g) garlic powder
salt and freshly ground black pepper
2 (60 g) whole eggs
1 cup (125 g) seasoned breadcrumbs
2.2 lbs. (1 kg) chicken breasts, cubed
canola oil, for frying
dipping sauce, for serving

Method
1. In a plastic bag, mix the flour, garlic powder, and some salt and pepper.
2. Whisk the eggs with 2 tablespoons water in a bowl.
3. Place the breadcrumbs in a separate shallow bowl.
4. Shake the chicken pieces in the bag to coat.
5. Dip each in the egg, then coat with breadcrumbs.
6. Heat enough oil in a deep frying pan over medium-high flame.
7. Fry the chicken in batches until golden brown then place on a plate lined with paper towels to drain the excess oil.
8. Serve with your favorite dipping sauce.

Nutritional Information:
Energy - 305 kcal; Fat – 11.4 g; Carbs – 22.5 g; Protein – 26.2 g; Sodium – 315 mg

Turkey Bacon Muffins with Chives

Preparation Time: 10 minutes; **Total Time:** 30 minutes; **Yield:** 12 servings

Ingredients
2 oz. (60 g) turkey bacon, cooked and crumbled
2 cups (250 g) all-purpose flour
1 Tbsp. (15 g) granulated sugar
2 tsp. (8 g) baking powder
1/2 tsp. (2.5 g) kosher salt
1/4 tsp. (0.5 g) freshly ground black pepper
2 tsp. (4 g) garlic powder
2 Tbsp. (7 g) chopped chives
1/4 cup (30 g) Parmesan cheese, finely grated
1/2 cup (60 g) sharp Cheddar cheese, grated
1 large (60 g) egg, beaten
1/2 cup (125 ml) skim milk
1/2 cup (125 g) sour cream
1/2 cup (125 ml) canola oil

Method
1. Pre-heat your oven to 400°F (200°C).
2. In a large bowl, mix all dry ingredients then set aside.
3. In a separate bowl, whisk together all the wet ingredients then gradually add to the dry ingredients until well-combined.
4. Spoon into lightly greased muffin tins.
5. Bake in the preheated oven for 20-25 minutes or until a toothpick comes out clean. Let cool on wire rack.
6. Serve and enjoy.

Nutritional Information:
Energy - 225 kcal; Fat – 13.9 g; Carbs – 18.8 g; Protein – 6.2 g; Sodium – 155 mg

Les Ilagan

Zesty Meatballs with Parsley

Preparation Time: 12 minutes; **Total Time:** 30 minutes; **Yield:** 8 servings

Ingredients
2 (60 g) whole eggs
3/4 cup (60 g) breadcrumbs
4 Tbsp. (30 g) Parmesan cheese, grated
3 Tbsp. (45 ml) olive oil
2 Tbsp. (30 ml) lemon juice
1 tsp. (5 g) lemon zest, finely grated
1/4 cup (15 g) fresh parsley, chopped
3 cloves (9 g) garlic, minced
1/2 tsp. (2.5 g) salt
1/4 tsp. (0.5 g) freshly ground black pepper
2.2 lbs. (1 kg) lean ground beef
canola oil, for frying

Method
1. Combine the eggs, breadcrumbs, parmesan, oil, lemon juice, zest, parsley, garlic, salt, and pepper in a large bowl. Mix thoroughly.
2. Add the ground beef and mix until combined well. Form mixture into 1-½-inch diameter meatballs.
3. Over medium-high flame, heat oil in a large pan. Then add the meatballs; fry until golden brown and cooked through, turning as needed to cook all sides evenly.
4. Transfer to a serving dish. Serve and enjoy.

Nutritional Information:
Energy - 349 kcal; Fat – 20.7 g; Carbs – 5.9 g; Protein – 33.9 g; Sodium – 314 mg

SOUTHERN COOKING

Egg on Avocado Boat

Preparation Time: 10 minutes; **Total Time:** 30 minutes; **Yield:** 4 servings

Ingredients

2 (200 g) ripe avocados, pitted and halved lengthwise
4 (60 g) large eggs
kosher salt
freshly ground black pepper
3 (1 oz. or 30g) slices of turkey bacon
chopped fresh parsley, for garnish

Method

1. Preheat oven to 350°F (175°C).
2. Place avocado halves in a baking dish, then crack 1 egg into each hollow part of the avocado then add pepper and salt.
3. Bake until the egg whites are set, and yolks are no longer runny, about 15 to 20 minutes
4. Meanwhile, in a large pan over a moderate flame, cook turkey bacon until crisp, about 7 minutes.
5. Drain oil by transferring to a plate lined with paper towels.
6. Chop bacon. Place on top of avocados along with chopped parsley.
7. Serve and enjoy.

Nutritional Information:
Energy - 304 kcal; Fat – 25.3 g; Carbs – 9.0 g; Protein – 12.3 g; Sodium – 434 mg

Les Ilagan

DESSERTS

Pecan Pie with Honey and Cinnamon

Preparation Time: 15 minutes; **Total Time:** 40 minutes; **Yield:** 10 servings

Ingredients
1 cup (340 ml) honey
3 (60 g) whole eggs, beaten
1/4 cup (60 g) butter
1 tsp. (2 g) cinnamon, ground

1 pinch nutmeg, ground
1 cup (100 g) pecans, coarsely chopped
1 (9-inch) single pie shell

Method
1. Preheat oven to 350°F (175°C).
2. In a medium saucepan bring honey to a boil. Cool slightly.
3. Whisk the eggs, butter, cinnamon, and nutmeg into the honey.
4. Stir in the pecan nuts. Pour mixture into the pie shell.
5. Bake for 25 minutes or until completely set. Cool slightly before cutting.
6. Serve and enjoy.

Nutritional Information:
Energy - 351 kcal; Fat – 18.8 g; Carbs – 44.6 g; Protein – 4.3 g; Sodium – 189 mg

Ultimate Pineapple Upside-Down Cake

Preparation Time: 20 minutes; **Total Time:** 50 minutes; **Yield:** 10 servings

Ingredients
4 (60 g) whole eggs (separated)
1 stick (125 g) butter
1 cup (220 g) packed light brown sugar
1 (20 oz.) can sliced pineapple
10 maraschino cherries (halved)
1 cup (125 g) cake flour

1 tsp. (4 g) baking powder
1/4 tsp. (1.5 g) salt
1 cup (220 g) white sugar
1 Tbsp. (15 g) butter, melted
1 tsp. (5 ml) pure vanilla extract

Method
1. Preheat oven to 350°F (175°C).
2. Over very low flame, melt butter in an oven-proof skillet or pan. Then, add the brown sugar and remove from heat. Cover bottom of the skillet with pineapple slices. Place cherry halves in the middle of each pineapple slice, cut side up. Set aside.
3. Sift together salt, baking powder, and cake flour.
4. In a large bowl, beat egg whites with an electric mixer until soft peaks form. Add white sugar slowly, beating well after each addition. Continue beating until medium-stiff peaks form.
5. In a small bowl, beat egg yolks at high speed until very thick and pale yellow.
6. Using a wire whisk or rubber scraper, gently fold egg yolks and flour mixture into whites until just blended. Fold in 1 tablespoon melted butter and vanilla extract. Pour batter and spread evenly over pineapple in the skillet.
7. Bake until surface springs back when pressed lightly with the fingertip and a toothpick inserted in the middle comes out clean for 30 minutes. Allow cake to cool a bit before inverting onto a large plate. Cut into 8 or 10 slices.

Nutritional Information:
Energy - 195 kcal; Fat – 8.2 g; Carbs – 28.6 g; Protein – 4.4 g; Sodium – 306 mg

Les Ilagan

Homemade Peach Crumble Cake

Preparation Time: 15 minutes; **Total Time:** 40 minutes; **Yield:** 8 servings

Ingredients

6 cups (900 g) ripe peaches, peeled and sliced
1/4 cup (55 g) packed brown sugar
3 Tbsp. (20 g) all-purpose flour
2 tsp. (10 ml) lemon juice
1/2 tsp. (2.5 g) lemon peel, grated
1/2 tsp. (1 g) cinnamon, ground
vanilla ice cream, optional

Crumbled Topping:
1 cup (125 g) all-purpose flour
1 cup (220 g) light brown sugar
1 tsp. (4 g) baking powder
1/4 tsp. (1.5 g) salt
1/4 tsp. (0.5 g) nutmeg, ground
1 (60 g) whole egg, lightly beaten
1 stick (125 g) butter, melted and cooled

Method
1. Preheat oven to 380°F (190°C).
2. Place the peaches in a lightly greased shallow baking dish (2-½-qt.).
3. Mix together the brown sugar, flour, lemon juice, peel and cinnamon in a small bowl. Sprinkle this mixture over the peaches.
4. Combine the flour, light brown sugar, baking powder, salt, and nutmeg. Whisk the egg in until the mixture looks like coarse crumbs. Sprinkle over the peaches. Drizzle with butter evenly over topping.
5. Bake in the oven for 35-40 minutes. Cool slightly.
6. Serve with ice cream, if desired.

Nutritional Information:
Energy - 309 kcal; Fat – 13.4 g; Carbs – 47.2 g; Protein – 4.1 g; Sodium – 171 mg

Luscious Lemon Meringue Pie

Preparation Time: 12 minutes; **Total Time:** 40 minutes; **Yield:** 8 servings

Ingredients
1 cup (220 g) white sugar
3 Tbsp. (20 g) cornstarch
2 Tbsp. (15 g) all-purpose flour
1/4 tsp. (1.5 g) salt
1 ½ cups (375 ml) water
1/2 cup (125 ml) lemon juice
1 Tbsp. (15 ml) lemon zest, finely grated
2 Tbsp. (30 g) butter
4 egg yolks, beaten
1 (9-inch) pie shell, baked
4 (40 g) egg whites
6 Tbsp. (90 g) white sugar

Method
1. Preheat oven to 350°F (175°C).
2. Over medium-high heat and in a medium saucepan, boil together lemon filling by mixing together 1 cup sugar, flour, cornstarch, and ¼ teaspoon salt. Stir often. Stir in butter. Place egg yolks in a small bowl and slowly whisk in ½ cup of the hot filling mixture. Transfer resulting mixture into the saucepan. Again, bring mixture to a boil and continue to cook while stirring constantly until it becomes thick. Remove from heat. Pour mixture into baked pie shell.
3. Prepare the meringue by beating egg whites in a large bowl until foamy. Gradually add while beating until stiff peaks form. Spread the meringue mixture over filling, sealing the edges.
4. Bake in the preheated oven for 10-12 minutes, or until meringue is golden brown. Cool before cutting.
5. Serve and enjoy.

Nutritional Information:
Energy - 359 kcal; Fat – 12.9 g; Carbs – 59.2 g; Protein – 5.3 g; Sodium – 290 mg

Les Ilagan

Mississippi-Style Mud Pie

Preparation Time: 30 minutes; **Total Time:** 30 minutes; **Yield:** 8 servings

Ingredients

2 cups (200 g) graham cracker crumbs
1/4 cup (55 g) brown sugar
1/2 cup (125 g) butter, softened
1 container (12 oz. or 340 g) frozen whipped cream, thawed
3/4 cup white sugar
1 (8-oz. or 250 g) cream cheese, softened
1 package (3.9 oz. or 110 g) instant chocolate pudding mix
1 package (3.4 oz. or 96 g) instant butterscotch pudding mix
3 cups (750 ml) milk
1 cup brownies or chocolate cookies, cut into small pieces

Method

1. Combine the graham cracker crumbs, ¼ cup brown sugar, and butter in a mixing bowl. Press the resulting mixture firmly in a 9x13 inch baking dish. Set aside.
2. Beat together half the whipped topping, ¾ cup white sugar, and cream cheese in a separate bowl then spread it on top of the crust.
3. Mix together the pudding mixes and milk in another bowl; spread on top of cream cheese mixture. Finally, top with remaining whipped topping and cookies. Chill until ready to serve.
4. Enjoy.

Nutritional Information:

Energy - 460 kcal; Fat – 24.2 g; Carbs – 54.7 g; Protein – 6.3 g; Sodium – 594 mg

Easy Blueberry Cobbler Ala Mode

Preparation Time: 20 minutes; **Total Time:** 1 hour; **Yield:** 6 servings

Ingredients
3 cups (450 g) fresh blueberries
3 Tbsp. (45 g) white sugar
1/3 cup (85 ml) fresh orange juice
2/3 cup (85 g) all-purpose flour
1/2 tsp. (2 g) baking powder
1/4 tsp. salt

1 stick (125 g) butter, softened
1/2 cup (110 g) white sugar
1 (60 g) large egg
1 tsp. (5 ml) almond extract
vanilla ice cream (to serve)

Method
1. Preheat oven to 380°F (190°C).
2. Combine blueberries, white sugar, and fresh orange juice in an 8-inch square baking dish. Set aside.
3. In a small bowl, mix the flour, baking powder, and salt together until blended well. Set aside.
4. In a medium bowl, beat butter and ½ cup sugar until light and fluffy. Mix in egg and almond extract. Add flour mixture bit by bit, stirring just until ingredients are incorporated. Pour the prepared batter over blueberry mixture. Spread to cover as much of blueberry filling as possible.
5. Bake in the oven until the top is golden brown, about 40 minutes.
6. Remove from heat then allow to cool on a wire rack prior to cutting.
7. Top with a scoop of vanilla ice cream and enjoy!

Nutritional Information:
Energy - 378 kcal; Fat – 18.6 g; Carbs – 50.9 g; Protein – 4.2 g; Sodium – 236 mg

Gooey Pecan Tarts

Preparation Time: 15 minutes; **Total Time:** 1 hour 55 minutes; **Yield:** 48 servings

Ingredients
1 cup (250 g) butter, softened
6 oz. (180 g) cream cheese, softened
2 cups (250 g) all-purpose flour
4 (60 g) whole eggs
2 cups (440 g) packed brown sugar

1 cup (340 g) honey
1/4 cup (55 g) butter, melted
1/4 tsp. (1.5 g) salt
1 tsp. (5 ml) pure vanilla extract
1 cup (100 g) pecans, coarsely chopped

Method
1. Prepare the crust by mixing the butter and cream cheese well.
2. Add flour and mix thoroughly. Divide dough into 4 portions and chill for at least an hour.
3. Meanwhile, prepare the filling by combining the eggs, sugar, honey, butter, salt, vanilla extract, and pecan nuts in a large bowl. Mix well. Set aside.
4. Preheat oven to 350°F (175°C).
5. Using a sharp knife, cut each dough into 12 pieces. You should get 48 pieces for the 4 dough portions. Roll each dough and press into the small muffin tin, covering all the way up to the edge.
6. Fill the tart shells with the pecan mixture, about 2/3 full only. Place pecan tarts in an ungreased baking sheet.
7. Bake for about 30 minutes or until lightly browned. Remove from the oven and let them cool for about 5-7 minutes.
8. Serve and enjoy.

Nutritional Information:
Energy - 138 kcal; Fat – 7.9 g; Carbs – 16.2 g; Protein – 2.3 g; Sodium – 63 mg

Key Lime Pie Home-Style

Preparation Time: 20 minutes; **Total Time:** 10 hours 45 minutes; **Yield:** 8 servings

Ingredients

2/3 cup (85 g) dry roasted slivered almonds
1 cup (100 g) graham crackers (crushed)
1/4 cup (55 g) brown sugar
1 pinch salt
1/2 stick (60 g) butter, melted

4 (60 g) large egg yolks
1 (14 oz.) can sweetened condensed milk
1/2 cup (125 ml) key lime juice
3/4 cup (185 g) cold heavy cream
1/2 tsp. (2.5 g) lime zest (finely grated)

Method

1. Preheat oven to 350°F (175°C).
2. Ground almonds finely in a food processor then add graham cracker crumbs, sugar, melted butter, and salt. Pulse again to mix well. Transfer mixture into a 9-inch pie plate and press to cover up to the edge.
3. Bake the crust in the oven for 10-13 minutes, or until golden brown.
4. In a large bowl, beat together egg yolks, condensed milk, cream, and lime zest then whisk in lime juice gradually to thicken the custard. Pour the custard into the baked pie crust and put back into the oven.
5. Bake for another 15 minutes to allow the custard to begin setting. Cool completely on wire rack. Loosely cover with plastic wrap and chill overnight.
6. Serve and enjoy.

Nutritional Information:
Energy - 387 kcal; Fat – 21.8 g; Carbs – 43.2 g; Protein – 8.0 g; Sodium – 197 mg

Crispy Fried Apples with Cinnamon

Preparation Time: 15 minutes; **Total Time:** 30 minutes; **Yield:** 8 servings

Ingredients
1/2 cup (60 g) all-purpose flour
1 pinch salt
2 Tbsp. (30 g) white sugar
1 tsp. (2 g) ground cinnamon
1/4 cup (60 ml) milk
2 (60 g) large eggs, beaten

1 ½ tsp. (7.5 g) lemon zest, finely grated
2 (180 g) green apples
2 Tbsp. (30 ml) coconut oil
1 Tbsp. (15 g) butter
powdered sugar (to serve)

Method
1. In a large bowl, combine the flour, salt, sugar, and cinnamon together.
2. Gradually pour in milk, stirring until it makes a smooth batter.
3. Stir in eggs and lemon zest.
4. Remove core and peel the apples, then cut into thin rounds. Dip apple slices in batter to coat.
5. Heat both oil and butter in a large skillet over medium heat. Cook apples until golden brown, turning once.
6. Transfer to a serving dish. Sprinkle with powdered sugar.
7. Serve warm.

Nutritional Information:
Energy - 273 kcal; Fat – 13.2 g; Carbs – 36.5 g; Protein – 6.3 g; Sodium – 103 mg

Quick and Easy Banana Pudding

Preparation Time: 25 minutes; **Total Time:** 25 minutes; **Yield:** 20 servings

Ingredients
1 package (5 oz.) instant vanilla pudding mix
2 cups (500 ml) whole milk (cold)
1 (14 oz.) can sweetened condensed milk
2 tsp. (10 ml) pure vanilla extract
1 container whipped topping frozen but thawed
1 (16 oz.) package vanilla wafers
14 ripe bananas (sliced)
whipped cream (for topping)

Method
1. In a large mixing bowl, beat pudding mix and milk for 2 minutes using an electric mixer.
2. Add the condensed milk and vanilla extract until smooth. Gently fold in the whipped topping.
3. Make a layer of wafers, pudding mixture, and bananas in individual dessert cups or glass jars. Top with whipped cream.
4. Keep it chilled and covered until ready to serve.
5. Enjoy.

Nutritional Information:
Energy - 331 kcal; Fat – 11.0 g; Carbs – 54.9 g; Protein – 5.3 g; Sodium – 434 mg

Les Ilagan

Blackberry and Cream Dessert with Honey

Preparation Time: 20 minutes; **Total Time:** 20 minutes; **Yield:** 4 servings

Ingredients
1 cup (250 g) all-purpose cream
1 cup (250 g) cream cheese, softened
1/4 cup (80 ml) honey
1/2 tsp. (2.5 ml) pure vanilla extract
3 cups (450 g) blackberries
fresh mint (for garnish)

Method
1. Using an electric mixer, beat together cream and cream cheese until smooth. Add the honey and vanilla extract.
2. Make two layers of cream mixture and blackberries in 4 glasses or serving cups. Garnish with fresh mint. Chill until ready to serve.
3. Serve immediately and enjoy.

Nutritional Information:
Energy - 279 kcal; Fat – 15.6 g; Carbs – 33.1 g; Protein – 4.7 g; Sodium – 193 mg

Watermelon Peach and Blackberry Salad

Preparation Time: 15 minutes; **Total Time:** 15 minutes; **Yield:** 4 servings

Ingredients
2 cups (300 g) watermelon (cut into small pieces)
2 cups (300 g) blackberries
2 cups (300 g) peaches, peeled and diced
fresh mint sprigs

Method
1. Place watermelon, blackberries, and peaches in a salad bowl. Toss to combine.
2. Keep it chilled and covered until ready to consume.
3. Enjoy.

Nutritional Information:
Energy - 83 kcal; Fat – 1.4 g; Carbs – 20.5 g; Protein – 2.3 g; Sodium – 2 mg

Les Ilagan

Chocolate and Vanilla Pudding

Preparation Time: 15 minutes; **Total Time:** 15 minutes; **Yield:** 5 servings

Ingredients

melted butter, to grease
1 cup (125 g) self-rising flour
1/2 cup (50 g) powdered sugar
3 Tbsp. (20 g) cocoa powder

1/2 cup (125 g) heavy cream
1/4 cup (60 g) butter, melted
1 (60 g) large egg, lightly beaten
whipped cream, to serve

Method

1. Preheat oven to 350°F (175°C). Brush 4 ramekins with melted butter to lightly grease.
2. Mix together the self-rising flour, powdered sugar, and cocoa powder in a medium bowl then make a well in the center.
3. Combine the cream, butter, and egg in a large jug. Slowly pour this mixture into the flour mixture and stir well. Transfer into the prepared dish and smoothen the surface with a spatula.
4. Bake in the oven for about 25 minutes, or until tested done (a cake-like top should form, and a toothpick inserted halfway into the center comes out clean). Cool slightly.
5. Serve topped with whipped cream.

Nutritional Information:

Energy - 317 kcal; Fat – 18.8 g; Carbs – 34.3 g; Protein – 5.3 g; Sodium – 89 mg

Baked Strawberry and Almond Crumble

Preparation Time: 10 minutes; **Total Time:** 30 minutes; **Yield:** 5 servings

Ingredients
1 lb. (450 g) fresh strawberries, hulled and halved
1/3 cup (35 g) powdered sugar
3/4 cup (95 g) all-purpose flour
1/4 cup (55 g) brown sugar
1/4 cup (60 g) butter, softened
1/3 cup (40 g) slivered almonds
whipped cream, to serve

Method
1. Preheat oven to 400°F (200°C). Lightly grease 5 (5 oz.) ramekins with butter.
2. Place strawberries and powdered sugar in a medium bowl. Toss to coat. Divide among 5 ramekins.
3. Combine flour, brown sugar, and butter in a separate bowl. Mix until mixture resembles breadcrumbs.
4. Add the slivered almonds. Stir to combine. Divide this mixture equally and place over strawberries, pressing dough together with your fingers.
5. Bake for 15 minutes, or until the top is golden brown and crisp.
6. Serve with whipped cream.

Nutritional Information:
Energy - 309 kcal; Fat – 16.7 g; Carbs – 38.4 g; Protein – 4.2 g; Sodium – 73 mg

Apple Cobbler ala Mode

Preparation Time: 10 minutes; **Total Time:** 30 minutes; **Yield:** 10 servings

Ingredients
6 medium (1.092 kg) Granny Smith apples, peeled then sliced thinly
1 cup (220 g) granulated sugar
1 cup (250 ml) cold water
1 Tbsp. (7 g) cornstarch
1 tsp. (5 ml) pure vanilla extract

1 cup (125 g) all-purpose flour
1 cup (220 g) brown sugar, packed
3/4 cup (75 g) rolled oats
1/2 cup (120 g) butter, melted
1/2 cup (60 g) walnuts, chopped
1/2 teaspoon (1 g) ground cinnamon

Method
1. Preheat an oven to 350°F (180°F). Grease a 9x13 inch baking dish.
2. Spread out the sliced apples in the prepared baking dish. Whisk together the granulated sugar, water, cornstarch, and vanilla extract in a small saucepan. Cook over medium heat until the syrup becomes clear, and sugar is dissolved, about 5 minutes. Pour hot syrup over the apples. Set aside.
3. Mix together the flour, brown sugar, rolled oats, melted butter, walnuts, and cinnamon until it forms a crumbly mixture. Place on top of the fruit mixture. Spread to make an even layer.
4. Bake in the preheated oven until the top is brown and bubbly, about 1 hour.
5. Serve warm and enjoy.

Nutritional Information:
Energy - 393 kcal; Fat – 13.7 g; Carbs – 67.9 g; Protein – 4.1 g; Sodium – 72 mg

Apple Fritters with Cinnamon

Preparation Time: 12 minutes; **Total Time:** 30 minutes; **Yield:** 8 servings

Ingredients
1 cup (125 g) all-purpose flour
2 Tbsp. (30 g) granulated sugar
2 tsp. (8 g) baking powder
1/2 tsp. (1 g) ground cinnamon
pinch of salt
1 (60 g) whole egg

1/2 cup (125 ml) whole milk
1 tsp. (5 ml) vanilla extract
4 (80 g) apples, chopped
canola oil, for frying
1 tsp. (2 g) cinnamon + 2 Tbsp. powdered sugar, for dusting

Method
1. In a large bowl, mix well salt, cinnamon, baking powder, sugar, and flour.
2. In a small bowl, lightly beat egg, milk, and vanilla.
3. Gradually add the vanilla mixture into the flour mixture. Combine well before stirring in apples.
4. Over medium heat and in a large non-stick pan, heat oil.
5. Drop 3-4 tablespoons of batter to the heated pan with oil and cook until golden brown on both sides. Transfer to a paper towel-lined plate.
6. Serve sprinkled with cinnamon-sugar mixture.

Nutritional Information:
Energy - 207 kcal; Fat – 8.2 g; Carbs – 31.8 g; Protein – 3.1 g; Sodium – 90 mg

Les Ilagan

Baked Pumpkin and Caramel Pie

Preparation Time: 10 minutes; **Total Time:** 30 minutes; **Yield:** 10 servings

Ingredients

2 cups (225 g) pumpkin puree
1/4 tsp. (1.5 g) kosher salt
1 tsp. (2 g) ground cinnamon
1/2 tsp. (1 g) nutmeg
1/2 tsp. (1 g) ginger, grated
1/2 tsp. (1 g) allspice

1/2 tsp. (1 g) ground cardamom
2 (60 g) whole eggs
1 can (400 g) sweetened condensed milk
1 (10-inch) ready-made pie crust
1/2 cup (170 g) dulce de leche or thick caramel sauce, warmed

Method

1. Preheat your oven to 400°F (200°F).
2. Combine pumpkin, salt, cinnamon, nutmeg, ginger, and allspice in a medium saucepan over medium heat. Cook until pumpkin is heated through, then transfer into a mixing bowl and cool slightly.
3. Add the condensed milk and eggs to pumpkin, whisk until it becomes smooth. Pour mixture into the prepared pie crust; top with dulce de leche or caramel sauce, spreading to create an even layer.
4. Bake in the preheated oven for 15 minutes, then reduce oven temperature to 350°F (175°C) and continue baking until a knife inserted 1" from crust comes out clean, about 30 to 35 minutes.
5. Allow to cool in a wire rack before slicing then serve and enjoy.

Nutritional Information:

Energy - 334 kcal; Fat – 13.5 g; Carbs – 47.7 g; Protein – 6.9 g; Sodium – 307 mg

Banapple Fritters

Preparation Time: 10 minutes; **Total Time:** 30 minutes; **Yield:** 4 servings

Ingredients
1 (180 g) apple
1 (150 g) banana
2 (60 g) whole eggs
1/2 cup (60 g) all-purpose flour
1/2 tsp. (1 g) baking powder
2 Tbsp. (30 g) brown sugar
1 tsp. (2 g) ground cinnamon
coconut oil, for frying

Method
1. Over medium-low flame, heat oil in a non-stick pan.
2. Remove the core from the apple and slice into ¼ inch rounds.
3. In a medium bowl, mash the banana with a fork well.
4. Add eggs to the mashed banana and mix until well incorporated.
5. Add the flour, baking powder, cinnamon, and brown sugar. Mix well.
6. Dip each apple slice into banana batter.
7. Cook 4-5 minutes on each side or until golden brown then arrange into a plate lined with paper towels.
8. Serve and enjoy.

Nutritional Information:
Energy - 231 kcal; Fat – 9.7 g; Carbs – 32.8 g; Protein – 5.3 g; Sodium – 38 mg

Les Ilagan

Carrot and Walnut Cake

Preparation Time: 10 minutes; **Total Time:** 30 minutes; **Yield:** 12 servings

Ingredients
1/2 cup (125 ml) canola oil
1/2 cup (100 g) applesauce
1 ¼ cups plus 1 tablespoon all-purpose flour (160 g)
1 ½ tsp. (6 g) baking powder
1 ½ tsp. (3 g) ground cinnamon
1/2 tsp. (2.5 g) kosher salt

1/2 cup (60 g) walnuts, coarsely chopped
3 (60 g) whole eggs
1 cup (220 g) sugar
2 tsp. (10 ml) vanilla extract
2 cups (250 g) carrots, grated
1 Tbsp. (15 g) brown sugar

Method
1. Preheat oven to 350°F (175°C).
2. Mix together flour, baking powder, cinnamon, and salt in a large bowl. Toss walnuts and remaining 1 tablespoon flour in a small bowl.
3. Using an electric mixer on medium-high speed, beat the eggs and sugar in another medium bowl until light and fluffy, about 4 to 5 minutes. With the mixer running, gradually pour in the oil, applesauce, and then the vanilla. Add this mixture into the dry ingredients and mix until just combined. Fold in walnuts. Transfer into lightly oiled and floured 9x5-inch loaf pan. Sprinkle with brown sugar.
4. Bake cake in the preheated oven until a tester inserted into the center comes out clean, about 65–75 minutes.
5. Allow to cool slightly before transferring to a wire rack.
6. Serve and enjoy.

Nutritional Information:
Energy - 258 kcal; Fat – 13.5 g; Carbs – 31.5 g; Protein – 4.3 g; Sodium – 128 mg

Choco Almond Cake

Preparation Time: 10 minutes; **Total Time:** 30 minutes; **Yield:** 10 servings

Ingredients

1 stick (120 g) butter, melted
8 oz. (250 g) dark chocolate, melted
4 (60 g) whole eggs, separated
1 tsp. (5 ml) vanilla extract
1 Tbsp. (15 ml) espresso powder

1/2 tsp. (2.5 g) kosher salt
3/4 cup (90 g) granulated sugar
1 ½ cups (180 g) almond flour
1/2 tsp. (2 g) baking powder
powdered sugar, for sprinkling (optional)

Method

1. Preheat oven to 350°F (175°C).
2. In a medium bowl, whisk together the melted butter, melted chocolate, 4 egg yolks, espresso, vanilla, and salt until blended well. Set aside.
3. In a large mixing bowl, beat the egg whites until it becomes frothy. Gradually add the sugar while beating until egg whites form stiff peaks.
4. Fold in the almond flour and baking powder. Gently stir in the chocolate mixture.
5. Pour batter to a greased 9-inch cake pan and bake in the preheated oven for 25-30 minutes, or until the middle of the cake barely wiggles. Let cool.
6. Sprinkle with powdered sugar before serving.
7. Serve and enjoy.

Note: Make sure not to overbake to avoid the cake from getting dry.

Nutritional Information:
Energy - 319 kcal; Fat – 25.4 g; Carbs – 17.0 g; Protein – 7.5 g; Sodium – 228 mg

Les Ilagan

Choco-Hazelnut Cookies

Preparation Time: 10 minutes; **Total Time:** 30 minutes; **Yield:** 24 servings

Ingredients
1 stick (125 g) unsalted butter, softened
1 ½ cup (180 g) granulated sugar
2 (60 g) whole eggs
1 tsp. (5 ml) vanilla extract
2 ¼ cups (280 g) all-purpose flour

3/4 cup (90 g) unsweetened cocoa powder
1 tsp. (6 g) baking soda
1/2 tsp. (2.5 g) kosher salt
1 cup (150 g) hazelnuts, chopped

Method
1. Preheat oven to 350°F (175°C).
2. In the bowl of a stand mixer fitted with a paddle attachment, beat together the butter and sugar on medium-high speed until light in color and fluffy, about 3-4 minutes. Gradually add eggs while mixing. Then, add the vanilla.
3. In a separate mixing bowl, mix together the flour, cocoa powder, baking soda, and kosher salt. Then gently add to the wet mixture in the stand mixer. Mix on low speed until combined well. Fold in the chopped hazelnuts.
4. Take a rounded tablespoon of mixture and place onto lined cookie sheet; repeat for remaining mixture.
5. Bake in the preheated oven until cookies are firm and cracked on top, about 10 minutes. Let cool on a wire rack.
6. Serve and enjoy.

Nutritional Information:
Energy - 156 kcal; Fat – 6.6 g; Carbs – 23.5 g; Protein – 2.8 g; Sodium – 136 mg

Chocolate Avocado Pudding

Preparation Time: 12 minutes; **Total Time:** 30 minutes; **Yield:** 6 servings

Ingredients
2 large avocados - peeled and diced
1/2 cup (60 g) unsweetened cocoa powder
1/2 cup (110 g) brown sugar
1/3 cup (85 g) skim milk
1 tsp. (5 ml) vanilla extract
1 pinch ground cinnamon

Method
1. Place the avocados, cocoa powder, brown sugar, skim milk, vanilla, and cinnamon in a blender. Process until smooth.
2. Divide among 6 dessert cups. Keep chilled and covered until ready to serve.
3. Enjoy.

Nutritional Information:
Energy - 204 kcal; Fat – 14.0 g; Carbs – 22.2 g; Protein – 3.0 g; Sodium – 16 mg

Les Ilagan

Country-Style Pecan Pie

Preparation Time: 12 minutes; **Total Time:** 30 minutes; **Yield:** 8 servings

Ingredients
3 (60 g) whole eggs
3/4 cup (165 g) granulated sugar
1 cup (340 ml) cane syrup
2 Tbsp. (30 g) unsalted butter, softened

1 Tbsp. (7 g) all-purpose flour
1 tsp. (5 ml) vanilla extract
1 cup (125 g) pecans, coarsely chopped
1 unbaked pie crust

Method
1. Preheat oven to 350°F (175°C). Prepare the pie crust by placing it into an ungreased, 9-inch pie plate and fluting the edges.
2. Whisk the eggs and sugar then stir in syrup and butter. Mix well.
3. Add the flour and the vanilla extract; mix well and fold in the pecans then pour into pie crust.
4. Bake for an hour in the preheated oven or tested done. Cover outside edges of the pie with aluminum foil about halfway through cooking to prevent overbrowning. Remove from heat. Let cool before cutting.
5. Serve and enjoy.

Nutritional Information:
Energy - 382 kcal; Fat – 24.2 g; Carbs – 38.1 g; Protein – 5.3 g; Sodium – 226 mg

Creamy Pasta and Fruit Salad

Preparation Time: 12 minutes; **Total Time:** 30 minutes; **Yield:** 8 servings

Ingredients
1 ½ cups (375 g) mayonnaise
¼ cup (60 ml) apple cider vinegar
1 Tbsp. (15 g) sugar
½ tsp. kosher salt
4 cups (560 g) macaroni noodles, cooked
1 lb. (450 g) boneless, skinless chicken breasts, cooked and chopped
1/2 medium (55 g) onion, chopped
1 cup (125 g) celery, chopped
2 cups (250 g) pineapple tidbits
2 (180 g) red apples, cut into thin small strips

Method
1. In a large bowl, whisk together mayonnaise, apple cider vinegar, sugar, and salt.
2. Add the remaining ingredients. Toss to combine.
3. Keep it chilled and covered until ready to serve.
4. Enjoy.

Nutritional Information:
Energy - 356 kcal; Fat – 14.9 g; Carbs – 37.9 g; Protein – 19.8 g; Sodium – 546 mg

Les Ilagan

Home-Style Apricot Galette

Preparation Time: 12 minutes; **Total Time:** 30 minutes; **Yield:** 8 servings

Ingredients

1 square sweet short pastry, approx. 30cm x 30cm
2 cups (250 g) canned apricot halves, drained
2 Tbsp. (30 ml) orange juice
1 tsp. (5 g) orange zest
1/2 tsp. (1 g) ground cinnamon
2 tsp. (5 g) corn flour
5 Tbsp. (75 g) brown sugar
1 (60 g) whole egg, beaten

Method

1. Preheat oven to 350°F (175°C).
2. Sprinkle some flour on a lined baking tray and lay the pastry.
3. In a medium bowl, mix together the apricots, orange juice, orange zest, cinnamon, corn flour, and 3 Tbsp. brown sugar. Then, place in the center of the pastry, leaving a border of about 1 ½-inch.
4. Fold the border of pastry over the fruit, leaving a large portion of the fruit uncovered, and gently make a few pleats. Brush the border with the beaten egg. Sprinkle with remaining 2 Tbsp. of brown sugar.
5. Bake in the oven until golden for 15 minutes.
6. Remove from the oven and let stand for a few minutes before cutting.
7. Serve and enjoy.

Nutritional Information:

Energy - 207 kcal; Fat – 8.1 g; Carbs – 32.6 g; Protein – 2.1 g; Sodium – 184 mg

Peach Cobbler ala Mode

Preparation Time: 10 minutes; **Total Time:** 30 minutes; **Yield:** 12 servings

Ingredients
4 cups (600 g) sliced peaches
1 cup (220 g) granulated sugar, divided
1 stick (120 g) butter
1/2 cup (60 g) all-purpose flour

2 tsp. (4 g) baking powder
1/4 cup (60 ml) whole milk
vanilla ice cream, to serve

Method
1. Combine peaches and a ½ cup of granulated sugar; let stand 15 minutes or until a syrup form.
2. Melt butter at 350°F (175°C) oven in an 11x7-inch baking dish.
3. Stir together milk, baking powder, flour, and the remaining ½ cup sugar. Place mixture over melted butter. (DO NOT STIR)
4. Add the peaches over mixture.
5. Bake in the preheated oven for an hour then serve warm paired with vanilla ice cream.

Nutritional Information:
Energy - 382 kcal; Fat – 19.0 g; Carbs – 51.9 g; Protein – 3.8 g; Sodium – 139 mg

Les Ilagan

Thanks a lot for reading!

I hope you enjoyed all the recipes here.

I look forward to reading your feedback by posting your review.

For more great tasting recipes, feel free to browse all my published books on Amazon.

SOUTHERN COOKING

Printed in Germany
by Amazon Distribution
GmbH, Leipzig